Improving Your Body Image
Through Catholic Teaching

IMPROVING YOUR BODY IMAGE THROUGH CATHOLIC TEACHING

How Theology of the Body and Other Church
Writings Can Transform Your Life

John Aquaviva, PhD

TAN Books
Charlotte, North Carolina

Cover design by Caroline K. Green

ISBN: 978-1-5051-1424-9

Published in the United States by
TAN Books
PO Box 410487
Charlotte, NC 28241
www.TANBooks.com

Printed in the United States of America

Contents

Foreword

As a syndicated Catholic talk show host, best-selling Catholic author, and motivational speaker, I have the honor and privilege of being frequently asked to endorse books as well as write introductions or forewords. The requests are also humbling because backing a publication comes with a big responsibility. It is crucial for me to ensure that the author and his or her material is truthful to the teachings of the Catholic Church and has a good, clear, concise message that will make a difference in today's challenging world. That is why I was so interested in supporting Dr. John Acquaviva's work. I didn't know John from Adam, as the old saying goes, when he first contacted me, but right away his approach to the topic of body image struck a chord with me on a number of levels.

First, much of my work is dedicated to engaging the culture. I have been in the media for thirty-two years, with the majority of that time working on-air in the secular press. After having a strong reversion to my Catholic faith, I began to notice how the industry that I had idolized for so long was doing much more harm than good. It wasn't just the sensationalism; the "if it bleeds, it leads" approach to news was becoming more and more commonplace. It was the overall media climate, in terms of programming content, music videos, the extremely violent images, the over-sexualization of women and girls, and the never-ending emphasis on appearance. The media outlets were bombarding viewers, listeners, and readers with all kinds of messages—messages that were having a direct and often negative impact on their lives. I was so disheartened and frustrated that I decided to make my misery over the media a new ministry. My primary focus now is not to tell people to throw out their TVs or computers but to discern the messages they are receiving and to learn how to use the media wisely.

Second, John's book strikes not just a professional chord with me but an extremely personal one as well. Not only did I work in the secular media for more than three decades and see its effects on society, I also suffered from its effects on a number of levels. For a long time I bought what the media were selling about body image and the focus on self. As an adult, that influence led to a lot of poor decisions in my life. The influence actually began, however, when I was much younger. As a female tween growing up in the '60s and '70s, I was one of the first diagnosed cases of anorexia nervosa at the local children's hospital in suburban Detroit. This, of course, was before cable TV, satellite TV, the Internet, et cetera. And yet, because I struggled with my weight, I became obsessed with looking like my favorite TV stars: actress Susan Dey, well-known back then for her role on the popular ABC sitcom *The Partridge Family*. (Re-runs of the show are still televised, and the cast is featured on retro lunchboxes.) All the girls I knew wanted to look like the tall, pretty, and extremely thin brunette who had the awesome job of working beside one of the major heartthrobs of the day, David Cassidy. And I was no exception. Little did I know when I began my extreme dieting that I was modeling myself after a young woman who would also later admit to her own struggles not only with anorexia but also bulimia— all while she was appearing on *The Partridge Family.*

Back then we didn't have too many Dr. Acquavivas around to help us develop a healthy body image and lifestyle. As a matter of fact, there was very little the medical and psychological world knew about eating disorders in general. Even today, there are very few Catholic experts who can address this major issue plaguing so many from the physical as well as a faith perspective.

Finally, after many years back in the arms of the Catholic Church, I have learned that the Church *does* have the answers to all of the struggles and issues that life throws at us—yes, even the issues of body image and general health. After all, if we really believe in God as our Creator, who better to direct us in these areas than him? This is exactly what Dr. Acquaviva does with this book: he takes us to the heart of who we are and what we were meant to be. It is only from that starting point that we can begin to heal and offer hope to others struggling to find out, as it says in Psalm 139, just how wonderfully made we are, being made in the image and likeness of God.

—Teresa Tomeo

How to Use This Book

Before diving into this book, it's important to understand its structure and how it came to be.

The book is divided into two major parts. Part I is a standalone book that I wrote in 2014 and self published. Years later, it garnered the attention of the good people at Saint Benedict Press and TAN Books, who agreed to publish it. But in the years between its original self publication and it falling into their lap, I developed a series of short activities that reinforced the lessons in the book by inviting the reader (or readers) to take a more active approach to the content— activities like body image surveys, word association games, discussion questions, personal reflections, pop culture critiques, and more. This host of activities makes up part II. With the help of my publisher, we combined these two parts into the book you presently hold.

The entire book—both parts—can be for both individuals and groups. If an individual, he or she can simply read part I and then reflect on the activities alone in part II. However, I recommend this book for groups. The activities at the end are best utilized and will have the most impact if they are combined with fruitful discussion with a group of peers. Recommended group sizes are five to fifteen people, but any size is fine. It may be helpful to split groups up according to gender considering the sensitivities surrounding the issue of body image. As far as age, this book and the activities are generally meant for young people (and groups can be paired up according to age), but as we will soon see, people of all ages can suffer from poor body image, so older adults are welcome to form groups as well. More specific information on how to run a group session can be found at the start of part II.

If you are doing this in a group setting, it's recommended that each participant obtains the book a few weeks before a session is set to meet. Reading part I will help form discussion and participation in part II. However, the activities are not dependent upon anything in part I. It is just as helpful for the participants to show up at the session, join in the activities, then take the book home and read part I to reinforce what they learned in part II. In other words, pick whichever order you choose, but do try to complete both parts to get the maximum benefit and education on this most important topic.

However you engage with the content, either on your own or with a group, or in whatever order you choose, I pray that it will serve you well and draw you closer to God.

Preface

The media has convinced us that we can be physically perfect, and as a result, many have a preoccupation with appearance. And sadly for those many, the attempt at a beautiful face and a proportioned, well-toned body is a part of everyday life. However, since perfection is impossible, millions of men and women suffer from some form of body distortion. And more importantly, they think their body lacks beauty or relevance unless they are found attractive, sexy, or lean—or all three.

Results of that intense desire to "cure" body imperfections are easy to see: eating disorders, the constant change in exercise habits, the prevalence of cosmetic surgery, and steroid use by non-athletes—most of which are common in early adulthood. When a disproportionate amount of time and effort are directed at this, daily productivity and emotional and spiritual health are compromised. Excess worrying, spending vast amounts of money, and obsessively dieting or exercising will eventually harm every relationship in our lives, including the one with God. Despite sincere efforts to be free of this issue, too many adults lose the battle when trying to defeat it without God's help. And Catholics, even the faithful or well catechized, are not immune to this struggle.

Although not everyone experiences body dissatisfaction, nearly everyone knows someone who does, and probably all would welcome an improved understanding of the true meaning of the human body. This book can help with that. Each chapter is inspired by Theology of the Body—a series of lectures given by Pope St. John Paul II—Scripture, and the teachings of the Church, all of which are designed to improve our understanding of the body's purpose and can assist in healing our own body issues. Learning to value the Church's teaching as it relates to the body leads to a greater appreciation of this wonderful gift. Moreover, addressing this matter early in life may help avoid decades of frustration, pressure, and psychological trauma.

Despite my years as a physical educator and a faithful Catholic, it wasn't until I became aware of these teachings that I started to become as grateful for my body as God intended me to be. Becoming aware of this material has been a true blessing for me and can be for anyone who hears it.

As a college educator for almost twenty years, and having taken plenty of classes and attended numerous professional presentations in the area of health and fitness, I was always aware that body image issues were common. Like many teachers, I try to convey openness so that students feel they can trust me. And of all of the concerns young men and women bring to me, the one most frequently confided is body image issues. Through these students sharing such deep, private weaknesses and shame, the complexity and severity of this issue was made clear and I found that I developed a greater concern and empathy for them.

In retrospect, I feel I rarely had "good answers" for these students. I felt the best I could do was listen, show concern, and hope that the conversation would end in them saying something like, "But now, all of that is behind me and I'm in a much better place." But in reality, body image problems rarely just "go away." While age and wisdom sometimes help a person change, the effects of a poor body image can linger for decades. More importantly, there seems to be so little relief from the very things that trigger the problem. Among them are magazines, television, films, and conversations with others who struggle with the same issues.

A couple of years into my teaching career, I was offered an opportunity to address this matter firsthand. My then-employer, Roanoke College in Salem, Virginia, decided as part of the graduation requirement that all students must take one Intensive Learning (or May Term) course. The short time frame meant that it would be a three-week course, meeting four to five hours per day in the month of May. The college's goal was to have each instructor create a new, unique course that was only offered during this special term.

I chose to create a course called "Weight Loss, Weight Gain and Body Image." It was while teaching this course that I gained an even greater understanding into the body image crisis. Despite the passion I have for the field of physical education, and in particular exercise physiology, it is the subject of body image that fascinates me most. In fact, the class piqued my interest even before it began. The first time it was offered, school administrators told me that it filled to capacity quicker than any other course in that May Term. From the very start, the students in both out-of-class assignments and in-class discussions (in front of strangers) addressed their personal beliefs, struggles, and fears regarding body image simply because a venue was provided.

Like any teacher would, I gained a great deal of insight on this topic, but what changed most was my compassion toward the students. The names and faces differed from class to class, but the stories, struggles, and even pain remains unchanged. I became aware that these struggles must be shared by many other people outside the confines of a small college in Southwest Virginia, and my compassion quickly encompassed all of them too. Regardless, I felt this class was going to be my solution, at least in part, to the problem. Upon reflection, I may not have offered any type of solution at all, but would serve only as a provider of information.

Though many agree that raising consciousness alone can be helpful, healing a poor body image requires more than learning about the history of dieting, the psychology of body distortion, and the results of a few scientific studies on eating disorders. This book limits similar background information and purposely omits any discussion on the sometimes-necessary psychiatric help; that's because the real intent here is to shed light on God's intention of the body so that adults can see it as gift and as a means to gain salvation rather than to see it as an entity that must perfected.

In the opening chapters of part I, there will be a discussion of the broad scope of the body image crisis, and using Genesis as the foundation, there will be an introduction to an understanding of the body's purpose. Then, in the next two chapters, there will be a focus on body disorder regarding men and women, with both chapters leaning on the *Catechism* and on Pope St. John Paul II's teachings as a solution to the basis of our problem. There will also be a chapter explaining some of the common triggers of a negative body image.

The final two chapters, however, will make a sincere attempt at offering an answer to the problem. By addressing the most basic aspects of our Catholic faith—the sacraments and prayer, as well as a discussion designed to empower and encourage the reader—the hope is to provide spiritual as well as practical solutions to help lift the burden of body dissatisfaction.

PART I

Introduction

Be who you are and be that well.

—St. Francis de Sales

Shortly after giving a lecture in a recent college health course, a student confided in me about the struggles she encountered, three or four years before, in her first attempt at college. She had gone to an out-of-state university, and like so many young people, she discovered the freedom of college life was too much to handle. She was on the college's meal plan and couldn't resist the rich foods offered to her daily. She soon struggled with her weight.

But that was just the beginning of her ordeal. She developed an obsession with her body size and became overly fearful of additional weight gain. In time, she became anorexic. In the midst of this, her father became ill with cancer, and the prognosis was grave. Her life spiraled downward. Depression set in, and she started skipping class and virtually gave up on school. She turned to alcohol, then cocaine, then heroin. Her drug use peaked when she began to use cocaine and heroin simultaneously, a possibly deadly combination.

Eventually, after running out of money and energy to live the life of a drug addict, she cleaned herself up and started over. She refocused, returned to school, and created direction for her life. Following the completion of her story, I asked if she feared relapsing into drugs and alcohol. Without hesitation, she looked me in the eye and said, "No, not really. I fear going back to being anorexic."

This from a person who was addicted to hard drugs and lost almost everything, a person who quit school, and whose friends stole from her to subsidize their own drug habits, and a person who was abused by her supplier-boyfriend. Yet, her biggest fear was being tossed back into a world of body weight obsession, counting calories, and excessive exercise.

What causes such an obsession with our bodies? What creates the all too frequent thought of not being accepted and not being attractive when the right look, the right size, or the perfect weight cannot be attained? Further, is there a solution to such an epidemic? The good news is that experts are not giving up, and neither should we.

This issue has become so widespread that a professional journal, *Body Image*, has totally dedicated itself to this subject. It was created since over 50 percent of women and 33 percent of men suffer from some type of body distortion.[1] To put these percentages in perspective, let's use them in an example of your fellow parishioners at a typical Sunday Mass. If there are 250 women and 250 men in the congregation,

---

[1]   T. Cash, J. Morrow, J. Hrabosky, and A. Perry, "How has body image changed? a cross sectional investigation of college women and men from 1983 to 2001," 2004, *Journal of Consulting and Clinical Psychology*, 72, 1081–90.

this means that 125 of the women and 82 of the men have daily battles with the look of their bodies. Interestingly, the age of the parishioners would be irrelevant in this case since body dissatisfaction runs the spectrum of a lifetime.

However, the greatest impact is on young people. Almost all of the people who suffer from severe eating disorders such as anorexia or bulimia are in adolescence and early adulthood.[2] Such data is common and in abundance given that today's culture is a constant reminder of what everyone *but* God says we should look like. The blatant effort by our culture—in particular, the media—has taken its toll. Unless we begin to see our own bodies through the lens of God and allow him to determine our real value, we must concede that our soul and emotional health are in immediate danger. Thus, this leads us to one major point: we cannot conquer severe body dissatisfaction on our own, nor should we try.

So, what can this book offer you? As of now, there have been no aggressive efforts to address body image in relation to Scripture, the *Catechism*, or John Paul II's Theology of the Body.[3] This book uses all three. With these three sources, adults of any age are sure to gain a unique and powerful perspective on the meaning of the human body—something either not pondered until this point or something very different from what they *think* the human body is for.

---

2   E. Stice, and J. Ragan, "A preliminary controlled evaluation of an eating disturbance psychoeducational intervention for college students," 2002, *International Journal of Eating Disorders*, 31(2):159–71.

3   Pope John Paul II, *Theology of the body: Human love in the divine plan*, (Boston, MA: Pauline Press, 1997). (Hereafter, citations in the text will refer to the dates of homilies, preceded by TOB.)

The Catholic Church has been generous in its material on
this matter, and has designed these teachings to be heard
by everyone, not just its faithful. As you read on, you will
find that the words from these sources are truly universal,
and because the body image crisis has no boundaries, people
from every religion, gender, age, and economic status are
sure to find the Church's language empowering.

Regarding other books on body image, several exist and
most are masterful at supplying a much needed historical
perspective, intense research concerning the body dissatisfaction in all age groups, and in-depth discussions of the cul-
tural influences of this issue. And despite the author's slant,
each is successful in getting the reader to comprehend the
magnitude of body distortion. Still, few attempts have been
made to address body image from an angle at which true
healing can occur: through the Word of God.

To be clear, there will be no effort here to create the
definitive book on the body image crisis, its causes, and the
impact it has on so many men and women; that has been
done several times.[4] Nor is it the intention to redefine or
fully explain the teachings found in Theology of the Body,
since that has been done as well.[5] In fact, these pages only

4   S. Grogan, *Body image: understanding body dissatisfaction in men,
women and children*, (New York: Routledge, 1999); S. Bordo, *Unbearable weight: feminism, Western culture, and the body*, (Berkeley,
CA: University of California Press,1993); H. Pope, K. Phillips,
and R. Olivardia, *The Adonis complex: the secret male crisis of male
body obsession*, (New York: The Free Press, 1993).

5   Christopher West, *Theology of the Body Explained: A Commentary on John Paul II's "Gospel of the Body,"* (Boston: Pauline Press,
2003); Richard Hogan, *Theology of the Body in John Paul II: What*

contain a modest number of direct quotes from Theology of the Body, although it should be noted that the former pope's revolutionary teachings are the sole inspiration for this book. Also keep in mind that St. John Paul II directly linked his work to Scripture and the *Catechism*—both of which are heavily relied upon here.

Theology of the Body has gained popularity in some Catholic circles, but relatively few are familiar with it. And if they've heard it, it's quite possible they didn't completely understand it due to its richness in philosophy and theology. As a result, the primary intent of this book is to bring the basic concepts of these teachings to all adults, and to do so in a manner that directly applies them to everyday life, especially where body image is concerned.

Even though Theology of the Body teachings can be purchased as a book, our late and beloved pope did not have a book in mind, as it was based on a series of 129 fairly brief talks, all of which were presented in the first five years of his papacy. At the center of his message, John Paul II tells us that God created the body as a sign of his own divine mystery. This is why he speaks of the body as a theology, a way to come to know God. Further, in his Son, "God has revealed his innermost secret: God himself is an eternal exchange of love, Father, Son, and Holy Spirit, and he has destined us to share in that exchange."[6]

It Means, Why It Matters (Frederick, MD: Word Among Us Press, 2007); Anthony Percy, *Theology of the Body Made Simple* (Boston: Pauline Books and Media, 2006).

[6]   *Catechism of the Catholic Church* (CCC), 221.

Those familiar with Theology of the Body usually have heard or read about it in the context of marital love, but it covers a multitude of issues, including the corporal and spiritual purposes of the human body. While these teachings have always been highly acclaimed by theologians, it's only recently that they have surfaced to the general public, and only a few attempts have been made to relate the Theology of the Body to specific topics outside of marriage. In any case, the pope's message in these talks is unmistakable: an appropriate use of the body is at the core of God's divine plan.

When we look at a majestic mountain, a splashing stream, or a beautiful animal, we not only see them as the proof of God the Creator, we may view them as the pinnacle of his creation. These examples are indeed wonderful, but we often fail to see that God's greatest creation, the human person, is what we should be in awe of most. While everything that God has made says something about his greatness, nothing speaks more loudly or deeply than does the body.

The human person is the greatest revelation of God's existence. Every person since Adam and Eve has been created in God's image, and their bodies prove God's reality. The body is God's way of allowing us to express what lies in the soul. This is the great mystery, and can lead to questions such as, "How can we mirror God in this ever-aging, limited, and flawed body?" and moreover, "How can my Catholic faith directly impact the way I see my body?"

Without the answers to these questions, it seems to be our tendency to allow others to dictate the worth of our bodies. Indeed, with enough stimuli, anyone could surrender to that. The hope here is to educate and reshape the thoughts we have about our bodies so we can lead more productive and meaningful lives. But since there have been so many distractions that lead us away from the true meaning of our bodies, something is needed to draw us back. The answer lies within our Catholic faith.

Our faith is not designed to erase or ease life's challenges, including those that occur from a negative body image, but the faith is here to lift us when those challenges occur. This is why the Church offers us a small library of writings on the body and its purpose. With this, we can come to know God better and we can come to know why he made us. Our role in this is to take what the Church offers and embrace it.

CHAPTER I

In the Beginning, God Created Body Image

Love tends upward to God and is not occupied with the things of earth. Love also will be free from all worldly affections, so that its inner vision does not become dimmed, nor does it let itself be trapped by any temporal interest or downcast by misfortune.

—Thomas à Kempis

We often hear the question "What are you afraid of?" when we are being prompted toward self-reflection. Fear too often governs our actions and, for that matter, our lack of action, especially when we are unaware that it is motivating us. Consider the role that fear plays in how we view our bodies; the fear that is generated by TV and magazine ads, for example. The formula for TV ads is cunning, yet simple: "If you don't use our product, you won't be attractive, sexy, or masculine/feminine," or even, "you won't be loveable." In addition to weight loss methods, products for baldness, makeup and beauty campaigns, and perfume and cologne, this fear tactic is also used in reference to a variety of body parts, both male and female, that were unmentionable in public just a few years ago.

With a bombardment of such fear tactics, the advertising agency will probably succeed since they use a variety of effective strategies such as clever TV commercials, glossy magazine photos, imaginative Internet ads, and even emails sent to personal accounts. But the single most effective strategy used is *relentlessness*. With that, so many people eventually concede and make the purchase. The reason? We believe that the product might lead to happiness and contentment.

Consider this story of a young woman who told me about the pressure she felt to be thin in college and, in particular, the pressure of being in a sorority. On one occasion when she wanted a candy bar, she purposely put on a large sweatshirt, walked down to the next floor to the vending machine, bought the candy bar, put it under the sweatshirt, walked back to her room, locked the door, ate the candy bar, immediately put the wrapper in her pocket, walked down to the next floor's trash room, threw out the wrapper, and then returned to her room hoping no one noticed. All of this was to avoid being "caught" by her friends, mainly her sorority sisters, who she feared would think of her as too fat. Incredibly, fear led this girl to act as she did. She was scared of not being accepted and being seen as undisciplined—both of which are logical when constantly surrounded by thin, often beautiful, stylish women.

Our fear, as was with the sorority girl, is that we aren't good enough as we are. The fear for many people is that life will pass them by unless a certain body type or a particular level of beauty is attained.

And then the problem gets even worse. Fear can morph into pride, and pride or self-love—when most thoughts or acts are meant to serve ourselves—can stifle the human person's true purpose: to participate in self-giving love. Our goal is to avoid shutting down physically and spiritually. True love does not contain fear; in fact, perfect love denies fear (see 1 Jn 4:18).

So, if fear leads us to react badly, what should our attitude be? For the answer, let's look at God's plan for us in the beginning, when the human race was created. As most have been taught, the Genesis story does not provide us with an accurate, historical account, but communicates religious truths to assist in our understanding of God's intention for us.

God created man with two components: the spiritual and the physical. Both of these components were involved in the fall of man. Eve was the first to fall spiritually by listening to and being tricked by the serpent. But in order to fall spiritually, *the body must cooperate*. We then see the body follow suit: it was here for the first time that man and woman were ashamed of their bodies. "I heard the sound of you in the garden, and I was afraid, because I was naked; and I hid myself" (Gn 3:10). Before that point John Paul II says that Eve, although fallen, could have been restored since Adam still would have remained intact as her sinless partner. But as we know, Adam also fell, and this act of sin has carried us to current times.[7]

---

[7]   John Paul II, *The Theology of the Body*, (Boston, MA: Pauline Books and Media, 1997).

Before the fall, God declared that he liked what he had made. He saw his creation—man—and said it was good. Man was indeed the pinnacle of his creation. A living being to govern over all of God's other creations, and more importantly, man was created to reflect God in the world (see Gn 1:26).

As the *Catechism* tells us:

> The human body shares in the dignity of "the image of God": it is a human body precisely because it is animated by a spiritual soul, and it is the whole human person that is intended to become, in the body of Christ, a temple of the Spirit.
>
> Man, though made of body and soul, is a unity. Through his very bodily condition he sums up in himself the elements of the material world. Through him they are thus brought to their highest perfection and can raise their voice in praise freely given to the Creator. For this reason man may not despise his bodily life. Rather he is obliged to regard his body as good and to hold it in honor since God has created it and will raise it up on the last day.[8]

God created us with the intention to reflect the love he has for us and to share that love with others. When we look at our bodies and those of others, we should see God—and his mystery. However, the inception of sin produced pride, selfishness, and the thought that we are independent, instead

---

[8]   CCC 364.

of God's intention—to love and respect our body and to
view it as a true gift.

John Paul II explains that our physical being alone indicates the existence of God, or what he calls the "God Question."[9] God provides us the freedom to offer our bodies to
him as well as our hearts. *This* is the essence of his Theology
of the Body: the body is the true "sign" that God exists. It
makes seen what was until that point, unseen. God, being
pure spirit and not visible, wanted his love for us to be visible, thus he created the human body in his image (Gn 1:27).
Furthermore, the pope tells us that the use of our body to
love others is a way to reflect the trinity, and the appropriate
use of the body will glorify God.[10] We do this through our
work, play, and in love and service to one another.

It is through such language that the pope seeks to answer
two vital questions: "What does it mean to be human?" and
"How do I live a life in a way that brings true happiness
and fulfillment?" Our bodies clarify the mystery of our existence. John Paul II says, "The body, and it alone, is capable
of making visible what is invisible, the spiritual and divine.
[The body] was created to transfer into the visible reality,
the invisible mystery hidden in God from time immemorial,
and thus to be a sign of it. [The body] is the fundamental
fact of human existence."[11]

But certain advertisements, immodest fashion, television shows, and countless other images have distorted the

---

[9]   John Paul II, *Crossing the Threshold of Hope* (New York: Random
       House, 1995).
[10]   TOB 1/13/82.
[11]   TOB 2/20/80.

meaning of this gift. The body has become so objectified (that is, seeing the body as a sex object) that from the time we are very young, sometimes before the age of ten, we succumb to what *society* wants for our bodies, not what *God* wants. The body is often portrayed as anything but a gift. Instead, it is something used as a means to an end. It is used to sell a product or for the person to "sell" themselves, and sometimes it is done simultaneously.

Take the example of cheerleaders of professional sports teams. The common reasoning as to why we would need professional cheerleaders is that it improves team spirit, whereas women might suggest that accepting such a job is that they want to support their favorite team or that it pays well. The truth, whether it's admitted or not, is that they are being used *and* are doing the using. By taking this job, cheerleaders enter the cycle of body distortion since they are in a powerful way being used for their bodies, and yet at the same time, they and their employer are responsible for adding to society's distorted views on appropriate uses of the body.

Dressing in such ways will certainly attract or sustain male viewership (why they're hired), all while using that role to enhance their own self-worth or improve their financial standing (why they seek it out). And to complicate this matter further, the average male viewer secretly desires his girlfriend or wife to have similar attributes of the cheerleader; while the average female viewer sees or at least senses that she cannot be worthy unless she emulates that level of beauty herself. Therefore, accepting or creating this job has its consequences on society, and everyone involved must recognize they are culpable—at least to some degree.

It should be noted that without the "cheerleader effect" in place, the beauty/fashion industry, most magazines, pornography, et cetera all fail as a business. They rely on this competitiveness among women to endure. Revenue is generated for each as a result of women demanding to look not only *her* best but better than all other women. At the same time, these same businesses rely on the male to either apply pressure on the female to maintain that look or for women to continue to operate under the illusion that all men want perfection. And more recently, the same industries have been successful at implementing this notion to a male audience as well.

In either case, the justification is sinister and it further deepens the distortion of the body's purpose. In fact, these very attitudes provide the basis of a society filled with poor self-worth and a negative body image. Thus, the madness continues: one has dignity only if one attains physical beauty or can effectively attract the other.

Research has been clear in demonstrating that the more we are exposed to images of the "perfect body," the more we turn our thoughts, intentions, and energy toward making ourselves this form of perfection. Aggressively seeking the flawless body will put us on a dangerous road for two fundamental reasons. One, we become selfish. When something takes a lot of time and effort, other aspects of life will naturally be neglected. Specifically, there's a distinct possibility feeble efforts will be made to seek out God, thus disallowing the pursuit of what he has called us to do: serve him by caring for and loving one another. Ignoring the call of God means providing very little (or no) time to be a caring friend, teammate, sibling, or son/daughter. Few traits or habits are more effective at hauling us away from God than spending countless hours and emotional energy striving for the perfect body. Down this same road, other negative thoughts can be formed, such as becoming convinced that it's actually possible to be perfect.

Second, failing to seek out God leads to the feeling that we don't need him. Thinking that we don't need God—perhaps a normal thought for many of us—quite simply puts our salvation in jeopardy. It is vital to our spiritual well-being that we respect the power of desired perfection and acknowledge the role that God plays in helping us to defeat it.

Understanding and embracing this notion of vocation to love God and show that love through our actions toward one another can override the desires of pride and vanity and lead us to make efforts to meet the needs of others. Knowing and accepting our vocation will lead us to a life of unselfishness and true fulfillment. Identifying with these basic principles of Christian living is how we begin to understand God's mystery, that the human body is his greatest gift.

It is St. Paul who pleads with us to offer our bodies to God, to make them a living sacrifice, to make our experiences actual acts of worship (Rom 12:1). Without the physical body, we would be lacking in our ability to concretely show love. The physical acts of love not only bond us to one another, they bond us to God and unfold for us the full understanding of life's purpose.

Reflect on what John Paul II said about our vocation:

Each one of you too is confronted by the challenge of giving full meaning to your life, the one life you are given to live. You are young and you want to live. But you must live fully and with a purpose. You must live for God, you must live for others. And no one can live this life for you. The future is yours, but the future is above all a call and a challenge to "keep" your life by giving it up, by "losing" it—as the Gospel has reminded us—by sharing it through loving service of others. You are called to be witnesses of the paradox that Christ proposes. "He who loves his life loses it, he who hates his life in this world will keep it for eternal life" (Jn 12:25). And the measure of ready to love, to assist, to help—in the family, at work, at recreation—those who are near and those who are far away. Also your success will be the measure of your generosity.

You, too, be courageous! The world needs convinced and fearless witnesses. It is not enough to discuss, it is necessary to act! . . . Live in grace, abide in His love, putting into practice the whole moral law, nourishing your soul with the Body of Christ, taking advantage of the Sacrament of Penance periodically and seriously. Always consider, with seriousness and generosity, whether the Lord might not also be calling some of you.[12]

Let us not forget, either, the various gifts the body offers. For instance, we have been granted the ability to work, create

---

[12]   John Paul II, Purpose of Vocation, 1997.

art, play sports or other recreational activities, express sexual love, display affection and gratitude towards one another (embracing, kissing, etc.), and honor God (kneeling, genuflecting, singing, etc.). Each is an authentic gift and should be understood in that way. When being consumed with the immoral and unethical roles that society asks us to fill, it becomes easy to forget the simplicity in which we can use the body in very noble, dignified, and holy ways.

And remember, if God says it is good, it's good.

CHAPTER 2

Did Eve Think She Was Too Fat?

*To a great extent the level of any civilization is the level of its
womanhood. When a man loves a woman, he has to become
worthy of her. The higher her virtue, the more her character,
the more devoted she is to truth, justice, goodness, the more a
man has to aspire to be worthy of her. The history of civilization
could actually be written in terms of the level of its women.*

—Archbishop Fulton J. Sheen

A student in one of my fitness classes recently inquired
about some exercises for her thighs and stomach. I
showed her some exercises but also felt the need to explain
"spot reduction"—a common misconception that an exercise
will remove fat only from the area being worked—knowing
full well that she was hoping that spot reduction would help
her. She was clearly disappointed that I mentioned this concept. She then pinched what tiny bit of fat she had in her
stomach area and sheepishly asked the same question again,
hoping that a change in tone would alter my answer. "But
you have no real fat to lose," I said. She didn't speak, but her

reaction was memorable. She tilted her head to the side and just smiled ruefully, as if to say, "I know. But I can't help it." It seems that this young gal is yet another casualty in the war of I-will-be-truly-happy-if-I-can-only-get-thinner. And clearly she's not alone. Virtually all research shows that at least 50 percent of women are dissatisfied with their bodies, with some studies showing that number to be as high as 70 percent.[13] Unfortunately, body dissatisfaction at any age is not unique since women have been known to have some distress about body image until they are elderly.[14]

It is well documented that women in advanced societies such as America are not the only ones that suffer from body dissatisfaction. For example, females in Korea, Australia, and Great Britain have distress over this same issue.[15]

---

[13] T. Cash, J. Morrow, J. Hrabosky, and A. Perry, "How has body image changed? a cross sectional investigation of college women and men from 1983 to 2001," 2004, *Journal of Consulting and Clinical Psychology, 72*, 1081–90; L. Vartanian, C. Giant, and R. Passino, "Ally McBeal vs. Arnold Schwarzenegger: Comparing mass media, interpersonal feedback and gender as predictors of satisfaction with body thinness and muscularity," 2001, *Social Behavior and Personality, 29,* 711–24.

[14] M. Tiggeman and J. Lynch, "Body image across the life span in adult women: the role of self-objectification," 2001, *Developmental Psychology, 37* (2), 243–53.

[15] J. Jung and G. Forbes, "Body dissatisfaction and disordered eating among college women in China, South Korea, and the United States: contrasting predictions from sociocultural and feminist theories," 2007, *Psychology of Women Quarterly, 31*(4), 381–93; J. Sheffield, K. Tse, and K. Sofronoff, "A comparison of body-image dissatisfaction and eating disturbance among Australian and Hong Kong women," 2005, *European Eating Disorders Review, 13* (2)112–24; S. Grogan, *Body image: understanding body dissatisfaction in men, women and children*, (New York: Routledge, 1999).

Surprisingly, research on women in less-advanced cultures has shown signs of body dissatisfaction as well, but in different ways than we are accustomed. In most poor countries, thinness is equated to poverty, malnutrition, and disease, and not seen as advantageous in any way. Plumpness, in many of those same regions of the world, signals wealth, health, and prosperity.[16] In affluent countries such as the United States, where food is abundant and obesity is common, being overweight has a much different connotation. Any degree of obesity is a sign that the individual is not in control and hints that they don't value the rewards that slenderness brings.

But desiring thinness in Western culture is a relatively new phenomenon. For much of our country's history, middle and upper class men would shun tan and thin women, thinking them as the (outdoor) working class, and even peasants. In the early 1900s, a different mentality began to emerge when the United States moved from a rural, farming culture to an industrialized nation. As a direct result, physicians in the 1920s advocated that women be more conscious of weight gain, since higher body fat on women was thought to be "energy depleting" and suggested that being overweight was less than desirable for a growing, more sophisticated society.[17]

Even gentle comments from doctors on obesity, a comparatively small matter at the time, and the mass distribution of fashion magazines can be linked to the frenzy we see

[16]   E. Rothblum, "Women and weight: fad or fiction," 1990, *The Journal of Psychology*, 124, 5–24.

[17]   R. Gordon, *Anorexia and bulimia: anatomy of a social epidemic*, (Oxford: Blackwell, 1990).

today. In fact, it was during this period that women's magazines went from using pencil drawings to depict the latest clothing trends to color photographs with real women, and for the first time, such publications began to have a strong effect on female readers' body image.[18]

Further technological advances, such as motion pictures, had impact as well. The movie-viewer of the 1930s and '40s noticed a change from the much slender actress from the silent movie era to a more curvaceous look seen on screen performers such as Mae West and Lana Turner. Because it was all new and each was powerful in their own way, seeing shapely film stars along with the volumes of color photographs probably had a similar influence on that generation that the media has on women today.

In the late 1950s, the "sweater" models, such as Marilyn Monroe, Jane Russell, and Jayne Mansfield, became popular, and never did the country see such a stir over a specific body type. It was impossible for it to go unnoticed that they all were pretty, with large breasts and small waists. In essence, this was the birth of current desire for the Barbie-doll look.

And something else happened earlier in that same decade. In 1953, a then-unknown Monroe posed for the first issue of *Playboy* magazine. The editor of *Playboy* purposely omitted the date on the cover of that first issue since he was unsure whether there would be a second one. Little did he know! Even though the world had seen nudes before, in pictorials and paintings, it could be argued that things changed

---

[18]   S. Orbach, *Hunger Strike: The Aanorectic's Struggle as a Metaphor for Our Age*, (London: Penguin, 1993).

forever with that one issue of *Playboy*. This magazine single-handedly altered public opinion about naked women.
Nudity was no longer isolated to art or underground dirty
magazines.

Playboy led the charge for its readers to admire a woman's body for pleasure alone and purportedly did so in a
"classy" and somehow acceptable way. The result, of course,
was neither classy nor innocent. The effect this had on male
readers eventually created a major problem. Subconscious or
not, men would make known their expectations and desires
for all women to look like this. Thus, any developing negative body issues that existed in women at the time shifted
into hyper-speed, with no signs of slowing down. Simply
put, women know that men are desirous of the airbrushed
beauty, and not shockingly, out of their need to be wanted,
they strive for that same perfection.

The good news about all of this is that men don't wish or
expect women to be as perfect as women *think* they should
be.[19] But the bad news is the standards for beauty and perfection are still high. Despite the fact that men are culpable to
a degree, women may be their own worst enemy since they
have trouble avoiding the triggers that create such standards.
Reading fashion magazines and watching risqué TV appear
to be two examples that heighten women's own frustration

---

[19]   G. Huon, S. Morris, and L. Brown, "Differences between male
and female preferences for female body size," 1990, *Australian Psy-
chologist*, 25, (3) 314–17; R. Bergstrom, C. Neighbors, and M.
Lewis, "Do men find 'bony' women attractive? Consequences of
misperceiving opposite sex perceptions of attractive body image,"
2004, *Body Image, 1*, 183–91.

and anxiety about their own bodies, while at the same time fueling their competitive side. For some, the need to compete is so fierce that they evaluate themselves based not just on how many men they attract but how many or how well they attract men *away from other women.* The solution to such problems may not be solved by turning off the TV or putting down a magazine, but it's a good place to start.

So, why has obtaining a positive body image become such a difficult and complex issue for women? It appears that the need to have a flawless body stems from a distinctive combination of social, health, and economic factors (many of which will be discussed in chapter 4). But notable authors point to one major culprit: from about the age of ten, a variety of media outlets apply constant pressure to be thin and beautiful. The problem deepens, however, when women cling to the illusion that they can (or must) have it all—something that clever thirty-second TV commercials can do. Women have been convinced that they should be able to work, recreate, raise children, be a great spouse, *and* be perfectly attractive all at the same time. Yet, as most of us know when we try to attain it all, it is inevitable that something (or everything) will go wrong. Most often this leads to a feeling of being out of control. When all of those pressures converge on women, some respond with a need to master one of the few things that *can* be controlled: the body.[20]

Therefore, the woman's feeling of helplessness can be remedied if this "in-control" mechanism can be regained;

---

[20]   Grogan, (1999); S. Bordo, *Unbearable Weight: Feminism, Western Culture, and the Body* (Berkeley: University of California Press, 1993).

and often as a result, the intense desire to be (or stay) thin and attractive fully develops. Moreover, women learn from an early age that unattractiveness and an unhealthy body weight is associated with unhappiness, laziness, lack of discipline, and lower self-confidence, all which are perceived as harmful when trying to land a good job, find a good mate, or make friends with influential people.

Nevertheless, women's values have been so distorted that thinness is considered for many to be the highlight of all accomplishments. Consider what women say (aloud or to themselves) when a pretty, slender woman walks by: "I hate her." Hate, of course, is not really how she feels; instead, she has feelings of intense jealousy. The feelings of envy emerge since she sees the thin woman as in control and probably even wonders how the woman remains tiny despite the availability of appetizing foods. Unfortunately, women's obsession with their bodies does not stop and start with thinness. Worrying about the width of their hips, breast size, hair, height, and leg and derriere shape all add to the craziness.

All of this considered, it is vital that we make attempts to heal this monumental issue. So let's continue discussing, as we did in the first chapter, what the beginning of time has to do with this. In other words, there is a basis for our divorce from the Truth. St. John Paul II tells us that we became detached from the true meaning of the body as a result of the Fall. In the beginning, Adam and Eve were naked without shame. They both understood the meaning of the body and recognized it as a gift. And since there was no shame, or sin, Adam and Eve saw the body as God intended it, as pure goodness.[21] Therefore, Eve did not see herself as imperfect. Nor would any conflict arise about the shape, size, and uniqueness of her body.

The Garden of Eden, where humanity began, is also where body distortion began. Although God's plan for man, as represented by the body, is to unite us to himself and to each other, it is obvious that Satan has had his effect. His role is to be a divider, between each other and between us and God.[22] Satan's plan, when successful, means that we will be critical of ourselves and those around us, regardless of how we *really* look. Since God created women to be naturally attracted to men (and vice versa), there's a crisis when the woman does not see herself as attractive or neglects in some way to see her body as inherently good.

Genesis 3:16, where it reads "Your desire shall be for your husband, and he shall rule over you," may explain why a woman may see herself as unworthy. It could be suggested that this verse describes a woman's fear of being alone and unwanted, as well as her need to be physically appealing to men. By itself, the woman's craving to be desired is understandable since we all need human contact and all want to be loved. But it's problematic when these basic notions are combined with a poor body image, leading to efforts, sometimes extreme, to ensure the man's attention. Note the number of women who have numerous sex partners or who often dress provocatively in an effort to validate themselves as worthy. And as we will continue to discuss, such a preoccupation

---

[21]   TOB 1/7/80.
[22]   CCC 394.

and stated actions lead to a series of unhealthy behaviors that will keep us from building a stronger relationship with God.

The Great Deceiver is well aware of our need to grow closer to God and is greatly pleased when we turn something as innocent and good as being healthy and fit into an obsession. Fitness magazines and health club ads have helped disguise in their own way the difference between being healthy and being perfect. Sometimes the line between these two is blurred and confusion sets in, which may help explain the millions of women who suffer from eating disorders.

Some advertisers pride themselves as trying to promote health and fitness, but bombard the consumer with comments about obtaining the perfect body. Perfection, as most of us realize, is not related to health. We can be very healthy and fit and not meet any of today's criteria for perfection. Just about every woman is familiar with the magazine cover that mentions the word "health" or "fitness" directly next to the phrase "Build the Dream Body" or "Get Picture Perfect Abs." Read this enough times and it's easy to see how someone would start to believe that this is truth—and the way to happiness. Still, the fact remains: when we fail to see the difference between being healthy and being perfect is when we fail to see God's intention for us.

This is why our faith, and in particular our former pope, has been so helpful in this regard. John Paul II directly addressed the need to fully embrace God's plan for the body: "Man cannot live without love. He remains a being that is incomprehensible for himself, his life is senseless, if love is not revealed to him, if he does not encounter love, if he does not experience it and make it his own, if he does not participate intimately in it."[23] The pope stresses this because striving for the "dream body" would probably take us further away from our purpose of loving others, not closer to it.

Regardless of how God is calling us to serve him, it will require the physical body. St. Paul tells us that our bodily offering is a spiritual act of worship: "I appeal to you therefore, brethren, by the mercies of God, to present your bodies as a living sacrifice, holy and acceptable to God" (Rom 12:1). Thus, it is through a willingness to die to this affliction, as Christ died for us, and start over that we may fulfill the meaning of our existence. It is because of Christ that we can be restored to our original glory—when we were without shame and were living in peace with our bodies, others, and our God.[24]

And remember, if God says it is good, it's good.

---

[23]   John Paul II, Encyclical Letter, 4/10/79.

[24]   TOB 1/9/80.

CHAPTER 3

Would Adam Have Taken Steroids?

God has so adjusted the body, giving the greater honor to the inferior part, that there may be no discord in the body, but that the members may have the same care for one another. If one member suffers, all suffer together; if one member is honored, all rejoice together.

—1 Corinthians 12:24–26

In 1998, baseball sluggers Mark McGwire and Sammy Sosa were vying for the single-season home run record. After their respective games, they would often give press conferences to discuss what was going on—the home run race. The interviews were a similar scene of them sipping water, answering questions, and them bulging out of their T-shirts as if the shirt was meant for an adolescent. It was impossible to ignore the muscularity of both players, and specifically how much size they gained since they entered the league years earlier. They were both pure superstars, and often expressed admiration for each other, demonstrated on one occasion when they hugged gleefully on the field to

30

celebrate McGwire's record-breaking home run (which coincidentally occurred against Sosa's team).

Shortly after that, major league baseball began running television commercials that showed clips of home runs and young, attractive women screaming for the players. The theme of the ad was "Chicks dig the long ball." Baseball was back. The game was now riding high after its popularity had slumped to a low point just a couple of years before due to a player's strike.

The party, however, was short lived. McGwire and Sosa, along with so many other players, came under suspicion of using performance-enhancing drugs, as evidenced by the sudden rise in their power-related statistics and because of their now-famous before and after photos. Journalists and even casual baseball fans began to express doubt about their "natural" muscle growth and rise to superstardom, and the media started displaying two sets of photos of McGwire, Sosa, and eventually Barry Bonds (and others) of a then-current picture and one from a couple years before. The differences in their builds were apparent, as were the changes in their statistics. Something seemed very wrong. Players were caught cheating and baseball cracked down, ending what is now unofficially known as the "steroid era" of the game.

But the use of steroids is not confined to baseball players. There has been suspected steroid use, and convictions of their use, in the past few years by athletes of a variety of sports, including track and field, football, and tennis. Athletes, even the most notable ones, have been cast into the spotlight for the wrong reasons. Stories on the use of performance enhancing drugs, illegal in almost any professional and amateur venue, have riddled the pages of too many sports sections. In particular, muscle-building products such as anabolic steroids and human growth hormone have blossomed into a preferred supplement, and not just by professional or serious athletes.

The numbers indicating such supplement use among novice or amateur bodybuilders, non-athlete high school students, and every day "Joes" have grown. For instance, up to 11 percent of all high school seniors, many of whom are not athletes but are merely looking to improve their appearance, indicated they have taken steroids.[25] Further, as many as three million adult males have used steroids for non-medical or performance-enhancement purposes, most of whom are white, professional, and in their twenties and thirties.[26] That is, they just want to look better. Television ads like "Chicks dig the long ball" will do that.

Until recently, men have been asked to adhere to a couple basic sociological principles: provide a financially and physically stable environment for those around them. In other words, "Be a man." Due to pressures from outside sources, most of which have plagued women for years, a "man" had been redefined. Today's culture of constant advertising tells us that a man is defined by his overall physical attractiveness, as well as his sexuality and stamina in the bedroom.

---

[25]   J. Cohen, R. Collins, J. Darkes, and D. Gwartney, "A League of Their Own: Demographics, Motivations and Patterns of Use of 1,955 Male Adult Non-Medical Anabolic Steroid Users in the United States," 2007, *Journal of the International Society of Sports Nutrition*, 4:12.

[26]   National Institute on Drug Abuse (NIDA) (2000). About Anabolic Steroid Use. NIDA Notes, 15 (15).

In days gone by, boys would daydream about being comic book heroes or sports stars, and as adults, it was common for men to adopt role models that more realistically defined manhood. In years past, for example, actors such as Cary Grant, Jimmy Stewart, and John Wayne were conventional favorites due to their no-nonsense attitudes, seeming ability to always do the right thing, and their display of manhood, regardless of the variety of manners in which they showed it.

Today, men are not only expected to be emotionally strong and financially secure, they feel compelled, for the first time in history, to be extremely conscious of their looks. Although slender, even muscular, bodies have been idealized since ancient times (e.g., in the Roman Empire), these ideals failed to have an extensive emotional impact on today's man, since they have not experienced serious pressure from any source until recent times. This notable shift may have started with popular movies in the 1980s when actors such as Sylvester Stallone and Arnold Schwarzenegger stumbled into nearly every scene with bigger-than-average muscles, extremely low body fat, and no body hair.

While Schwarzenegger and Stallone graced the big screen shirtless many times, their characters were not so threatening since they were more action-figure-come-to-life than sex symbols that appealed to either gender on mass levels. However, Brad Pitt in the 1991 movie *Thelma and Louise* may have single-handedly changed things. He appears to be the first male actor in major motion picture history whose brief role will be remembered more for his looks and body than for his acting. In fact, there was a bedroom scene in which Pitt's toned body was so much the focus that it stunned some viewers. Many movie critics agreed this was something never really experienced by the movie audience until that point, at least not with a man. Because Pitt's character was seen as a sexual object, it was offensive to some, but others found it appealing. For the women who found it appealing, some were sure to make flattering comments about his body, and being overheard by (or said directly to) men adds to the man's anxiety over not being in better shape.

Also, in the 1990s, mainstream magazines began to slowly "undress" their male models by featuring them in nude or semi-nude pictorials. Women's fashion magazine readers have seen this for years with females, but it soon became the norm for male readers to see other males for more than a "pretty face" and the jacket, sweater, or shirt on their back. Their shirts came off, literally, and a large number of models were causing the male readers to become increasingly self-conscious about their own bodies. In addition, *Playgirl* magazine, as the authors of the book *The Adonis Complex* assert, had its own influence on men's body issues, as has *Playboy* for women. The authors have determined that by implementing a specific formula to the models from mid-1970s to the late 1990s, they became progressively more muscular *and* displayed a lower percentage of body fat. On those same models, there's also been a difference in body hair (less of it) and age (younger) since the 1970s.[27]

As a result, men are experiencing the strain to reach a certain level of attractiveness in both face *and* body, a clear

---

[27]   H. Pope, K. Phillips, and R. Olivardia, *The Adonis Complex: The Secret Crisis of Male Body Obsession*, (New York: The Free Press, 2000).

change from the standard desire to be handsome, rugged, or suave. And the statistics support this: the current level of men that have body dissatisfaction is 33 percent. Although this is still a much lower number than women at 50–70 percent, it's drastically higher than the 10 percent noted in the 1970s.[28]

It's now evident that the media has made the same impact on men as it has on women; it just took them a little longer to find out that there was a whole other gender on which to inflict this pain. As with the models in *Playgirl*, males on TV and in other magazines have become younger, more muscular, and have decreased in body fat, causing a reversal (of sorts) of anorexia, also known as bigorexia or muscle dysmorphia. Just as a woman may never see herself as thin enough although they have low body weight, men often feel that despite being in really good shape, they still don't look good enough. An example, albeit an extreme one, may best be seen in champion bodybuilders, who are not just muscularly built but downright enormous.

This all reverts back to one basic issue: fear. Men are, more than ever, growing in fear that they cannot be successful, sexy, handsome, or even a "regular guy" unless they look a certain way or achieve a particular body type. Despite all of the information on the dangers of using steroids, there seems to be a greater fear for some men of not meeting a certain muscular standard, and because of this, they are willing

---

[28]   T. Cash, J. Morrow, J. Hrabosky, and A. Perry, "How has body image changed? a cross sectional investigation of college women and men from 1983 to 2001," 2004, *Journal of Consulting and Clinical Psychology, 72*, 1081–90.

to take their chances with their use, or worse yet, may not even care about the negative outcomes. I remember one conversation when a student confided in me that he wanted to take steroids. He was an ordinary guy, not an athlete or an avid bodybuilder. I reminded him of the countless side effects *and* the fact that they are illegal, but all he wanted to know about was their effectiveness. We were like two ships in the night.

In a subtler matter than steroid use, the sale of men's cosmetic products has risen substantially, especially in the past decade. A glimpse at many of the TV commercials during a sporting event spells this out loudly. While there is nothing wrong or immoral with appropriate grooming or hygiene (or sound nutrition and fitness plans, for that matter), this all points in the same direction; that men are becoming increasingly more conscious of their looks, and thus need to consider if they are bordering on an obsession.

This obsession, as discussed in the previous chapter, began in the Garden of Eden. Prior to the serpent making his presence known, the Garden was a place of peace and harmony, and a place where Adam and Eve saw what God had made, their bodies, and agreed that they were good. Adam, in particular, would agree that any form of physical activity, including weight training, is also good for the body. Engaging in an exercise regimen shows that we care for our bodies and prefer to benefit from the variety of "rewards" that it brings, such as an increase in energy, a strong heart, and better sleep patterns, all of which are noble goals.

Our aim should never be to always associate exercise and developing a healthy, even attractive body with the possibility that perfection can or should be attained. Rather, look at employment, physical activity, sports, and all other ways that we can use our bodies as a way to live a fuller life, as well as to glorify God (1 Cor 6:20). Yes, we please God when we score a touchdown, get a base hit, or reach a new maximum bench press, as long as we accomplish it in an ethical manner *and* accept God as the creator of this fine machine. Actually, many athletes "get" this. Recall the number of occasions that you've heard an athlete thank God immediately after they have contributed to a big win.

Also, recognizing the body as being willed by God is one of the ways that we can acknowledge his love for us and truly be thankful for the opportunities he gives us. Failing to see that the body is God's instrument for the message of salvation is failing the see the most basic principle that God wants us to know: why we were born.[29]

While Adam would agree with St. Paul, who said that taking care of the body is wise since it houses the Holy Spirit (1 Cor 6:19), he would have certainly discussed body obsession if it were an issue in those days. Before the Fall, Adam would rightfully take care of his body and not abuse it or become absorbed with it in any way, including taking steroids. Further, any man untainted by original sin knew that too much time spent on attempts to perfect the body would be futile since nothing is perfect except God, and that it's not dignified since we are taking time away from investigating our real purpose of life, which is to constantly ask, "How can I serve the Lord today?"

---

[29]   TOB 2/20/80.

Once Adam sinned, however, his purpose and mentality changed. God told him, "In the sweat of your face you shall eat bread" (Gn 3:19), indicating that Adam must now labor for his food and fight for his very existence. From that moment forward, the man was referred to as the "hunter and gatherer." In addition to being responsible for providing for his family, the man has always been the traditional and literal protector of his family.

In fact, despite the technological advances that we've experienced, man's instincts remain so that he can be called upon to feed, defend, and do anything else that demands strength and stamina to care for his wife and children. This reveals that the man *should* be strong for a variety of reasons that are displayed in everyday tasks, but nowhere is it written that the man needs a flawless body to farm effectively or must have a full head of hair to tend to his family. That is, it's not necessary to be physically perfect to earn a good wage, to be an adoring husband, or to be a loving father. Thankfully, God created us to be inclined to do what is good, and if certain distractions are limited, our souls can remain wholesome. Thus, our role is to nurture the inclination toward the good by seeking out his will.

And remember, if God says it is good, it's good.

CHAPTER 4

Why the Hysteria?

*We live in a society whose whole policy is to excite every nerve
in the human body and keep it at the highest pitch of artificial
tension, to strain every human desire to the limit and create
as many new desires and synthetic passions as possible.*

—Thomas Merton, Trappist monk

A couple of years ago, when I created and taught the
course "Weight Loss, Weight Gain and Body Image,"
I spent a lot of time scheduling guest speakers for the class.
Some of the speakers included a plastic surgeon, a gastric
bypass surgery nurse, a registered dietitian for obese clients,
and an editor for a women's magazine. This magazine editor
spoke to my class on the first session. She talked to the students about Photoshop, a common software program that
most magazine editors use to manipulate just about everything found in a photo. For instance, they can remove a tree
from a picnic scene, make a dress a brighter shade of red, or
make the model look "better." Her talk to my class, at my
urging, focused on the latter.

She discussed in detail how editors, including herself, use this basic computer software to whiten teeth, remove veins from the white of the eye, improve imperfect skin, add muscle to a man, and decrease fat on a woman. She showed specific changes she made in the photos of her own magazine, as well as other (mainly fashion) magazines. She stated that while models are naturally attractive, none—at least in the way they appear in magazines—are as perfect as they seem. Her point was that the very models that the readers are desperately aspiring to emulate don't even exist.

The class, made up of traditional age college students (eighteen to twenty-two), was silent with awe throughout her presentation. I am sure the students had thoughts of everything from "She can't be serious" to "How long have we been duped?" But after a few more comments from the editor on this subject, one of the female students, in near tears, said, "Why do they do that to us?"

With that, I almost cried myself.

When I asked the editor to speak to my class, I knew the topic would be interesting, perhaps even fascinating, but I had no idea that it would stir so many feelings and trigger so many insecurities in the students. The reality was that her talk was honest and forthright, but also downright sad. The level of anguish in the question "Why do they do that to us?" is palpable. This question also provides insight into the depth of the problem that so many people have with their bodies. However, this "problem" is really more than a nuisance. It has become for too many a constant and dramatic life issue.

College professors, a variety of researchers, and countless number of concerned bystanders have identified the numerous factors that lead to a poor body image. Many of these factors are so powerful that they even challenge men and women who have an otherwise healthy view of themselves.[30] This is why the word "hysteria" is used in the chapter title. When one thing goes wrong, it's a problem, but when many things are out of control, there's a feeling of panic. Those who are fighting against an intense poor body image are doing so as if they are one soldier surrounded by a number of enemies, each with a different weapon firing at the soldier from every direction. The onslaught of firepower can simply be too much. Let's now take a look at some of the causes of this hysteria.

Magazines

If you were to do a quick survey of the dozens of men's and women's fashion or fitness magazines, it would be impossible to ignore the countless number of young, fit, often gorgeous models that occupy most of the space on each cover. Inside the pages of each of these magazines the onslaught of photos continues. The models are often wearing next to nothing, even though the product being advertised has no justification for such immodesty. In all cases there is a guarantee that no model will be anything but perfect, in both

---

[30]   S. Grogan, *Body Image: Understanding Body Dissatisfaction in Men, Women, and Children*, (New York: Routledge, 1999); S. Bordo, *Unbearable Weight: Feminism, Western Culture, and the Body* (Berkeley: University of California Press, 1993).

face and body. But look more closely. Even though they are striking, the models don't really look "normal."

Genuine up-close shots would reveal skin blemishes, veins in the white of the eye, skin pores, tiny (and not so tiny) facial hair, and some yellowness of the teeth. Yet, these photos don't show any of that. Is it possible that there are models that don't have pores or facial hair, or those that have perfectly white eyes and teeth? Is it possible that the modeling agency found the only humans on earth without any of these flaws? Of course not. And to no one's surprise, it's been theorized that readers, especially women, make comparisons of themselves to the models during the minutes/hours following the time spent with these magazines.[31]

Sure, it's natural to compare ourselves to others, but problems arise when we do. First, the reader will constantly compare themselves to something that doesn't even exist. How unfair is that? (Or even better, "Why do they do that to us?") Second, a barrage of images intensifies a poor body image. Just one glance at the cover of these magazines in the grocery store line can trigger such feelings, not to mention looking through the entire magazine, or moreover, subscribing to and reading them every month.

We now know that this problem affects men as well. The previous chapter makes reference to the fact that the male models in health, fitness, and fashion magazines have

---

[31]   B. Major, M. Testa, and W. H. Bylsma, (1991). "Responses to upward and downward social comparisons: The impact of esteem-relevance and perceived control," in J. Suls and T. Wills (Eds.), *Social comparison: Contemporary theory and research*, (Hillsdale, NJ: Lawrence Erlbaum, 1991) pp. 237–60.

increased in muscularity while they have decreased in fat and body hair. All of this in addition to the usual tanned, thick-haired, and attractiveness of the model can create a major insecurity for the male reader.

It's not just the model's bodies that have an effect either. Inspect these photos from a different perspective. The models are almost always happy, even joyful. Sometimes, there are others in the photo just as happy. When a woman is the focus, the man in the picture is often looking at the "cover girl" with affection, lust, even love, and certainly with approval. The same goes for many men's magazines where the women are in awe of him. This actually intensifies the problem. People looking at this will not only see the perfect body and face, but that supposedly *having* the perfect body and face is necessary to bring joy, affection, respect, and love. That is, if we attain bodily perfection, there will be true contentment.

Everyday Discussions

A somewhat secretive yet common topic of conversation among men and women is the fear and downright shame that they feel about their bodies. How that fear is expressed is different with each gender. For women, such conversations occur often but are avoided in specific situations, like perhaps when men are present. Men, as reported in the book *The Adonis Complex*, usually reveal such fears only to wives or longtime girlfriends, but not always.[32] Friends and

---

[32]   H. Pope, K. Phillips, and R. Olivardia, *The Adonis Complex: The Secret Crisis of Male Body Obsession* (New York: The Free Press, 2000).

family members tend *not* to be part of a man's comfort circle. Women, on the other hand, due to societal norms and natural characteristics, are more likely to discuss their fears to a wider group of people such as friends, family members, and even other women who they may not be close to but who they instinctively know have similar feelings, thus creating a bonding effect. In both cases, however, the conversation takes place when the atmosphere is "safe" and where they feel they will not be judged or ridiculed.

Under the right circumstances, each gender will discuss a wide range of fears and insecurities that they have about their bodies. Both genders express concern with weight, being too tall or too short, or simply not finding themselves attractive for a variety of reasons. Men, specifically, differ from women in that they also frown about not having enough muscle, or having too much hair in some areas (e.g., chest, back) and not enough in others (e.g., scalp). Fears isolated to women usually involve not being thin or pretty enough, having small breasts, and even having feet that are too big.

One of the most interesting facts about having such talks is that often the listener will be sympathetic and even denounce any discussion of their friend not being "good or pretty enough," but in turn will have a similar conversation with another friend about *their* insecurities. This creates a perpetual cycle of one doing the complaining while the other does the listening and comforting. This shows the power of a society filled with people who have a poor body image: a cycle is established despite the listener knowing that such conversations are harmful and full of non-truths. Yet the listener will soon become the complainer and never heed their own words from the previous conversation.

Though it may be harmless and even normal to periodically be a part of these discussions, it is the regularity of them that will cause long-term damage. Take, for example, a male or female who is average in body weight, muscle tone, and overall attractiveness, and has a relatively positive body image. If their friend, on the other hand, constantly complains about being too fat or voices other similar complaints, this dialogue may erode any good body image feelings that existed initially. This issue could be further complicated when the friend is widely considered to be attractive, since that could make anyone turn the magnifying glass on themselves.

Television

Since Americans devote so much time to TV-watching (e.g., most adults average two or more hours per day, most adolescents average four or more hours per day),[33] this is a major offender in increasing anxieties over the adult's body. While the effects of commercials, music videos, and soap operas play a part, the biggest culprit on TV might lie in the night-time programming, in particular the reality shows. Reality

---

[33]   S. Bowman, "Television-viewing characteristics of adults: correlations to eating practices and overweight and health status," 2006, *Preventing Chronic Disease, 3*, (2), 183–91; R. Anderson, C. Crespo, S. Bartlett, L. Cheskin, and M. Pratt, "Relationship of physical activity and television watching with body weight and level of fatness among children: results from the Third National Health and Nutrition Examination Survey," 1998, *JAMA, 279*, 938–42.

TV, which boasts dozens of programs about a variety of topics, claims some of the highest ratings. Further, many of these shows are designed for a young audience experiencing a time in life when issues about their own body image are just developing.

Here is the common formula for reality TV: The subjects, often contestants of some kind, are almost always young, attractive, and in good physical shape. To intensify the matter, they are almost always shown in less-than-modest clothes, a bathing suit, or various states of undress. To complicate things even further, some of the conversations or "interviews," more common among women contestants, revolve around competitive-type discussions on who is better looking or more likely to attract attention from their male counterparts.

All of this funnels to the same problem as previously mentioned: exposure to these images will eventually lead to comparisons. Unfortunately, this is a fight that cannot be won. In particular, a comparison to contestants who have been hand-selected for their youth and attractiveness is an inevitable crushing blow to the viewer's self-esteem, especially if the contestant on TV is successful or victorious in any way. Just as in magazine ads, these displays of success, victory, or happiness create the illusion of being content. Even though we tell ourselves that watching reality TV is for entertainment purposes only, the fact remains that they leave us with long-lasting images that play a role in creating a negative self-view.

Cosmetic Surgery

Here are some important numbers regarding plastic surgery in this country: In 2007, the American Society for Aesthetic Plastic Surgery reported 11.7 million cosmetic surgical and nonsurgical procedures were performed in the United States. That's over a 400 percent increase since 1997, when compilation of these statistics began.[34]

Breaking it down by gender, 2007 statistics from the same organization show that women had 91 percent of all surgical and nonsurgical procedures. Not surprisingly, the surgical procedures that women most often chose were breast reduction or augmentation, and the top nonsurgical procedure was Botox. Further, nonsurgical procedures have increased by 743 percent since 1997. Men only account for 9 percent of all procedures (tops were liposuction and Botox), but there was an astonishing 886 percent increase in nonsurgical procedures from 1997 to 2007.[35]

Such data make profound statements. There are a lot of procedures being done, and men are feeling increased pressured to improve themselves in ways that have long been only common among women. And considering that the numbers increase each year, there is every indication that this industry will continue to prosper. This creates a problem for a couple of reasons: 1) Making this somewhat routine or habit elevates the playing field. In other words, what was once for the elite, rich, older, or desperate, is now seen as anything from

---

[34] The American Society for Aesthetic Plastic Surgery (2008). Retrieved from http://www.surgery.org/press/news-release.

[35] Ibid.

acceptable to necessary; and 2) it will produce a keeping-up-with-the-Jones' mentality. Along the same lines as the power of magazines and TV, an illusion is created to the observer, thus increasing the pressure to be like someone that doesn't really exist, at least not naturally.

Dolls and Action Figures

A glance at this title and one might wonder, "How big of a problem could this be?" Well, it's not only a factor, but it may be the most powerful, albeit the most subtle one of them all. Like so many psychological problems of adulthood, whatever the issue, it's possible to attribute the problem to what we experience as children. This is the theory behind figurines that are popular with children.

It is now a widespread notion that Barbie is a major culprit in causing body disorders in women. It has been estimated, for instance, that if Barbie were to be an adult, her size and dimensions would be as follows: Her height would be 7' 2" and she would weigh 101 pounds; her shoe size would be a 5; her breasts would be a FF cup; and her waist would have the identical circumference of her head. It doesn't take an anatomy teacher to know Barbie suffers from a severe case of disproportionate disease. Though it's easy to pick on Barbie due to her popularity, numerous other doll makers continue to contribute to women's body disorders for similar products.

The effect that dolls have on women's body issues cannot be measured; it can only be theorized. But it is an interesting theory, and probably a correct one. From the time girls are young, sometimes before they can even talk, they play with dolls. Seeing and touching a doll that is beautiful, not to mention forever young, can only add to the hysteria, not take away from it.

Although it is difficult to imagine, action figures have probably contributed to male body disorder as much as any issue. The authors of *The Adonis Complex* were the first to devote several pages to this phenomenom.[36] One glance at today's action figures reveals that this is no subtle matter. The modern-day versions of these toys (Batman, G.I. Joe, and even the Star Wars heroes) are so muscular that the only difference between them and the world's largest, steroid-ridden bodybuilders is a cape, a mask, and colorful boots. In effect, these action figures reflect the growing pressures that men now deal with regularly: The desire to become more muscular, have almost no fat, and be void of virtually all body hair.

Fitness Apparel

In keeping up with the modern trend of immodest clothing, today's fitness apparel is extreme. It is designed in such a way that low body fat and defined muscles appear to be a prerequisite. These products are marketed as "superior athletic wear," and its purpose is to improve performance; however, the true appeal may be the "form-fitting" look that is "tight" and "revealing." These clothes can and do improve workouts in the cold and heat, but they can also increase an unrealistic expectation to be lean and shapely.

---

[36]   Pope, et al. (2000).

Competitive female athletes face additional challenges. Not only do the athletes have coaches who encourage them to become and remain very lean to improve competitiveness, the standard attire for some sports are clothes that are so revealing that the athlete has the pressure to look good, and even be sexy, *while* performing well. Therefore, it must be no shock that female athletes are more prone to eating disorders than the general population or even women who participate in moderate exercise.

Exercise physiologists have indeed determined a correlation between low body fat and improved performance for specific athletes such as gymnasts, figure skaters, volleyball players (beach or conventional), and those in track and field, but the clothing choices in these sports must be considered yet another factor for disordered body issues. The clothes are *not* modest, and in all-too-many sports, the skimpy apparel has become the norm and even an expectation, not the exception.

The fact is, we have the right to dress anyway we want. However, our rights need to be understood and implemented within a moral framework rooted in the dignity of the human person. Further, the Church teaches that with every right there are responsibilities.[37] So it's important to understand that we are responsible for the way we dress, whether it is for informal situations, athletic competition, or employment. Failing to heed the demands of modesty means we are contributors to the hysteria and directly ignoring

---

[37]   CCC 1914.

God's intention that the body be seen as an extension and reflection of him.[38]

Constant exposure to the above stated issues can have a duel negative impact. It's enough that these issues become a factor in how we judge ourselves, but it will lead us to a life of being critical of others as well. It's harmful in itself to lack appreciation of our own body, but the situation gets worse when we allow these factors to control how we see others, especially our mates. Needless to say, this will intensify any poor body issues that already exist in those we care about most. Expecting them to make body changes can only confuse them and ourselves on the real meaning of love.

Ogling the opposite sex in the form of TV and magazine ads, pornography, athletes, and cheerleaders will lead to unfairly comparing them to others, even the ones we care about most. It's inevitable, unfair, and ultimately dangerous to our spirit and theirs. That's why Pope John Paul II wrote that the theological meaning of the body is to be a "witness to love."[39] With a true belief in this, we can begin to conquer these powerful tools that lead us to the wrong understanding of the body's purpose.

In the opening chapter, a professional cheerleader was used to illustrate that we often forget or don't comprehend the body's purpose. The cheerleader, of course, was used as a metaphor for a variety of people, professions, and situations. Our culture genuinely struggles to identify the body with something good and useful to and for God. It's true that the

---

[38]   TOB 2/11/81.
[39]   TOB 1/9/80.

body can and should be used for sexual purposes—in the right circumstances, such as when a couple expresses marital love for one another—but the body is more than just physical.

Take, for example, when we look at the cheerleader, or a photo of a pretty woman or a handsome man. What we see tells a particular story, but it doesn't tell the complete story of that person. What can be seen is a pretty face, curves, muscles, and so on. What can't be seen, however, is a whole lot more. Our tendency is to ignore the fact that along with that body is a mind and a soul. And regardless of the intent of the advertisement or profession they are engaged in, that person deserves dignity and respect because God made them.

This chapter devoted some effort to identifying the triggers that lead to a poor body image. But such a discussion only solves one small part of this big problem. The purpose of this book was to go well beyond some of the causes of this issue. Therefore, the next two chapters are devoted to making a sincere effort to calming this storm. God did not make a mistake in creating our bodies, so by taking a deeper look at his intention, and particularly discussing the faith that he left through his Son, perhaps we can leave a life of body obsession in the past.

And remember, if God says it is good, it's good.

CHAPTER 5

Calming the Storm: How Our Faith Heals Us

Christ has no body now on earth but yours, no hands but yours, no feet but yours, yours are the eyes through which Christ's compassion is to look out to the earth, yours are the feet by which He is to go about doing good and yours are the hands by which He is to bless us now.

—St. Teresa of Avila

There's an old joke about faith: During a downpour, a man stays in his house despite a call for flooding. Eventually, the flooding gets so bad it storms into his house and he's forced to climb up on his roof. A man in a boat comes by to offer him a ride, but he turns the ride down, saying, "No, thanks. I have faith in God. He'll save me." Two more boats come by and he turns those down as well. Finally, a helicopter swoops in, but, you guessed it, he turns that down and screams over the hoofing of the blades, "No, thanks! God will save me!" But the man eventually drowns. When he gets to heaven, the man approaches God and asks, "I don't get it. I had faith in you. Why didn't you save me?"

Perplexed, God replies, "What do you think the boats and
the helicopter were about?"

Most find this joke somewhat amusing, but some see
that it offers a slightly deeper, spiritual meaning. God often
appears to us in ways that are non-eventful and even mun-
dane. But he *is* there, always reaching his hand to us. Our
responsibility is to reach back. Sometimes Catholicism gets
a "bad rap," particularly from its youth, but those who are
negative towards it may have never really "used" it. At the
core of our faith is its teaching, also known as the *Catechism*.
It is rich, well explained, reasoned, and offered to us daily, all
of which provides significance to our lives. But still, it is up
to us to engage in it and ultimately embrace it.

When we fail to see or accept God's grace, we fail to attain
the relationship that we're destined to have with him. We
receive those graces as a result of our Catholic faith. That's
why we're Catholic. We have been catechized to trust in
God, and in particular, to use what the Church offers—such
as prayer, the sacraments, and Holy Mass—as the means
to deepen our relationship with him and grow in likeness
to Christ. The previous chapters, perhaps interesting and
even insightful to many, would not by themselves be healing tools, thus leading the reader to this very section of the
book. Let's take a closer look at how Catholic faith can assist
in our efforts to heal the suffering of a poor body image.

Prayer

"Virtues are formed by prayer. Prayer preserves temperance.
Prayer suppresses anger. Prayer prevents emotions of pride

and envy. Prayer draws into the soul the Holy Spirit, and raises man to Heaven" (St. Ephraem).

Referring to the Gospel of John (8:32), I once heard a priest say, "There is freedom in honesty." The priest noted that being honest with ourselves and with God is a great way to begin any healing that needs to occur within us. By being honest in prayer, we acknowledge our strengths and weaknesses. In both of these we grow in humility, and humility leads us to a better, more meaningful relationship with God. Prayer helps us to cultivate that relationship. We are asked to pray for forgiveness, to give thanks and praise, and to petition, such as asking for spiritual, mental, or physical healing for ourselves and others.

Leading a life of acceptance and gratitude helps bring us to the peaceful state toward which we all strive. Expressing gratitude for what we have—for life itself, and for a body to live that life—is how we begin to develop that peace. A good place to start is frequent reflection on the previous chapters where the body is described as a gift—needed especially on those days when feeling beautiful or handsome, even in God's eyes, is difficult to fathom.

Still, every day we make an important choice: We can fill our hearts with gratitude *or* be a complainer. Perhaps God's greatest reward to those who are grateful is to bless them with more gratitude. Conversely, when we fail to recognize this gift, and to not be thankful for it, it is a failure to recognize God's love and thus we deprive ourselves of the very graces he wills us to have. In fact, some of our most rudimentary actions allow us to become closer to our Creator: being able to kneel, fold our hands, and head slightly forward are ways that we demonstrate that we are in prayer, making it obvious that this most basic form of communicating with God is greatly improved by means of the body.

When we understand the greatness of God's gift, we begin to understand his divine plan of salvation. If God formed us in the womb (Is 44:24), then there is a plan for each one of us. Being willed by God means that he wants us here, and our role is to determine why that is. It is through this understanding that we can be more thankful and come to fully realize what God asks of our bodies.

St. Paul tells us to avoid being overly concerned in all matters, but to give thanks and praise to God. Through prayer, he promises us that God's peace will be upon us because God transcends all understanding and will guard our hearts and minds in Christ (Phil 4:6, 7). In the anxious-ridden life of body obsession, peace may appear out of reach, and further, may be so powerful that it seems no one could possibly understand the depth of the problem. But God indeed does. He hears the cry of those who suffer and wants to help us (Job 24:28). God is not the last hope; he is *the* hope.

Consider a prayer like this as part of your daily communication with God:

> Lord, you know that I don't always like my body. And sometimes, I dislike it because it's not perfect. All of this worrying and complaining I do about my body is affecting the way I see and treat others, and it's keeping me from loving You the way I should. Lord, help me to accept the way you made me, and to turn my focus to serving others, as you intended me to do. I love you

for giving me a body that allows me to do so many things that are good, like hugging my friends and family members, playing my favorite sport, participating in the hobby I love, and reading a good book. I ask you God, to send your Holy Spirit upon me so I can fully appreciate this wonderful gift you have given me: my body. Amen.

It will always be a mystery how and when God responds to prayer, but we know that he does. We know that God answers prayer through our own experience, through the testimony of others, and through Scripture. But perhaps the most influential way is through our conscience. We were created to hear the voice of God, and that voice is constantly letting us know that he listens and that we can and *will* be healed. It is up to us to consistently bring ourselves before God on bended knees, with a humble tone, and to be direct in what we ask. Recall the fervor that Christ displayed in his agony at Gethsemane (Mt 26:36–39, 42, 44). Christ teaches us a great deal about prayer in those brief yet intense moments. At his most vulnerable time, he turns to his Father with all of the humility and passion that he can muster, and he prays.

"Every one who calls upon the name of the Lord will be saved" (Rom 10:13).

Confession

"For a constant and speedy advancement in the path of virtue, we highly recommend the pious practice of frequent confession, introduced by the church under the guidance of the Holy Spirit; for by this means we grow in a true knowledge of ourselves and in Christian humility, bad habits are uprooted, spiritual negligence and apathy are prevented, the conscience is purified and the will strengthened, salutary spiritual direction is obtained, and grace is increased by the efficacy of the sacrament itself" (Pope Pius XII).

You might know that confession is also referred to as penance or reconciliation, but few know it as a sacrament of healing and the sacrament of conversion. Let's briefly discuss both of these latter phrases in relation to those with a poor body image.

In one way or another, healing is what we need, and in particular, healing is essential when we struggle with body distortion. Few afflictions, especially when extreme, are more paralyzing to everyday life. Serious forms of body dissatisfaction cast us into a world where a variety of negative feelings persist. It's a world of self-absorption and unawareness, but also one of anxiety, fear, pain, sadness and forms of self-hatred. They all lead to a life of unhappiness and discontent. In such tough times, we have difficulty hearing God's voice, and we struggle with hearing and answering the needs of others.

God calls us to a life of holiness, and that includes the full acceptance of his gift to us—life itself as expressed through the body. Since man is sinful, the full redemption of the body will only be fulfilled by his own resurrection. John Paul II encourages a life of virtue, purity of heart, and to attain perfection on earth by a complete awareness of our own sinfulness,[40] therefore, we become more perfect and grow in holiness when we prostrate ourselves to the Lord and acknowledge our sins.

Although those with body distortion are victims, some fail to see that indulging in or perpetuating a poor body image can be sinful due to its damaging affect to ourselves and those around us. But it's easy to be blinded by this issue.

First, we are sinning against one another when we neglect to serve others, since our thoughts, time, and money are absorbed by the obsession. Second, dressing immodestly in an attempt to attract another or to feel worthy means we have lost the meaning of sex and the appropriate time to express it—in private within the context of marriage. The desire to feel sexy or to stir up lustful thoughts in others makes us an accessory to sin. Third, constant dialogue with friends about the poor view we have of our bodies may cause *others* to generate similar feelings about themselves. Lastly, we are sinning against God when we deny our body as a gift and fall into the dangerous notion that there is truth and dignity in, "If I have a nice body, there's reason to show it off," when in reality it's insecurity or a certain unawareness that leads to such behavior.

The sacrament of confession gradually peels away the barriers between sin and virtue, and allows us to be in full communion with God.[41] In this state, body distortion, self-ishness, and pride fade away. *This* is the grace of God at work. And this is how we are healed. The healing that occurs from

---

[40] TOB 12/9/81.

[41] John Paul II in Christopher West, *Theology of the Body Explained* (Boston: Pauline Books, 2003).

this sacrament brings us to a new understanding of God and his love. Love is what converts the heart into experiencing a new and joyful way of life.

Contemplate the very first quote from Christ in the Gospel of Mark: "The kingdom of God is at hand; repent, and believe in the gospel" (Mk 1:15). This is a call to conversion. Unlike the people of Christ's time who were in the infant stages of knowing the gospel, we have heard it but need to be reminded of it so we can remain in the way of Christ. Despite our level of education on the Faith, we are in constant need of purification and thus should seek the sacrament of penance regularly;[42] otherwise, we will continually be enveloped by society's definition of the purpose of the body and not God's.

"If we confess our sins, he is faithful and just, and will forgive our sins and cleanse us from all unrighteousness" (1 Jn 1:9).

Eucharist

"Receive Communion often, very often. . . . There you have the sole remedy, if you want to be cured. Jesus has not put this attraction in your heart for nothing" (St. Thérèse of Lisieux).

The greatest of all invitations is the one that Christ extended to us at the Last Supper. He offered us Holy Communion so we can be in union with him.[43] By accepting his invitation, we have the ability to experience God's peace by

---

42   CCC 1428.
43   CCC 1391.

separating us from sin and preserving us from future sin.[44] Our goal is to wipe away the burden of a poor body image and cure it with the Eucharist. What better way to cure our poor body image than with the Body of Christ!

As many of us know, the Eucharist means "giving thanks" or "thanksgiving," and this includes gratitude for redemption, freedom of sin, and for creation. In part, God made humans to have "dominion" over creation (Gn 1:26). Creation itself was made for and out of love for us.[45] This is a truly incredible gift in itself. And as with all gifts, we should be thankful for it and let our thanks be known. This is why we should seek the Eucharist. Love of one another, ourselves, and of God can falter in daily life, so we need this nourishment to die to the sin of body obsession and to live in such a way that expresses our debt to God for his great creation.[46]

In reference to regularly receiving communion, it reminds me of my old Hot Wheels playset (yes, the toy cars). Hot Wheels used to sell a small oval track for the cars to go around. But with it also came a garage-type section that contained two battery-operated spinning wheels to help the cars circle around the entire track. Each time, the cars would barely make it to the garage, only to be jetted around again. The Eucharist acts as those spinning wheels; it provides much-needed assistance when we need it most.

When we deny ourselves the Eucharist, we are denying this unique presence of Christ to help us battle everyday life. We want and need our Lord to remain in us, literally, to manage

---

44   CCC 1393.
45   TOB 1/2/80.
46   CCC 1394.

the barrage of TV ads, movies, music videos, and countless other distractions that can lead to a poor body image. Better yet, we need the power of Communion to help *avoid* those triggers and turn more consistently toward the good. In fact, Christ gives his solemn promise that he will be with those who eat his flesh and blood (Jn 6:56). We must trust in God that he will deliver those who seek him out. God knows the pain that body obsession brings; let us bring our pain to him so he can heal us as he promises.

Mass

"Hear Mass daily; it will prosper the whole day. All your duties will be performed the better for it, and your soul will be stronger to bear its daily cross" (St. Peter Julian Eymard).

"Protect us from all anxiety, as we wait in joyful hope for the coming of Our Savior, Jesus Christ." Just prior to the Great Amen (the conclusion of the Eucharistic Prayer in Mass), the priest says these words as a plea to God to pierce our hearts so that we may see that the bad times, sometimes frequent, will pass and the peace of Christ will be with us.

Many people who experience the stifling effects of a negative body image are in need of the peace that God has promised through his Son. At the center of the Catholic Church's life is the Mass.[47] It is here that we give thanks, ask for forgiveness, hear God's Word, and ask for strength from the Eucharist. In essence, it's what we've been discussing in this chapter. The celebration of the Eucharist—the Mass—is the culmination of our Faith and is ultimately a display of the

---

47   CCC 1343.

body's attempt to grow in communion with God. This is why the *Catechism* refers to the Eucharist as the source and summit of our faith.[48]

Since Christ is the full embodiment of God, this means that God can be seen, touched, and heard in the context of daily life. This principle is known as sacramentality, one of the defining characteristics of Catholicism. The Church regularly offers certain rituals, which we call sacraments, that make the presence of God tangible to us in a variety of ways. Sacraments are the mediator between God and his people, and such encounters are designed to deeply affect our lives. At the core of the sacraments is the Eucharist, and the Eucharist is at the core of the Mass.

Not only is it through the Mass that we can petition God for forgiveness and healing of our body issues, but it is through an understanding of how we use our bodies that will make us grow in appreciation for this gift. The Mass was instituted by Christ to allow our bodies to fully experience God through the use of the five senses. God has given us the ability to see, hear, smell, touch, and taste every aspect of the celebration. For instance, our encounter with Christ is enriched when we *see* the Host being raised, when we *hear* the Word of God, when we *smell* the incense, when we *touch* the Eucharist, and when we *taste* his Blood. Without these senses, in fact without our bodies, we cannot develop a relationship with God.

Let us never forget that we are willed by God. This means that from the moment of conception, God willed us to

---

[48]   CCC 1324.

know his Son in word and action, thus opening the gate of salvation. Following the Gospels points us in the direction of that gate.

The Gospels are celebrated every time we go to Mass. Further, accepting the invitation to actively participate in every aspect of the Mass brings us closer to God. In this life, the body and soul cannot be separated, for it is the physical body that allows participation, but it is our soul that reaps the benefit. This form of cooperation is not coincidental. If we were without one of them, salvation would not be possible.

I began this chapter with a joke about the man who refused to accept help during a flood. If we suffered from a poor body image for a lifetime, it's possible upon our death that we would go before God, like the man did, and ask why he didn't save us from years of agony. God would probably say something like, "What do you think the sacraments, prayer, and the Mass were about?"

God intended that we live with full appreciation of our bodies, and he certainly does not want us to experience any of the anxiety and pain that accompanies the lack of bodily perfection. Any pain, however, is the result of the Fall, and from that moment our need for God's grace has been intense. Due to God's gratuitous nature, we are blessed to have his grace constantly offered, although we must be willing and active participants in the process. The sacraments, the greatest gifts the Catholic Church can present, can be neglected or underappreciated, perhaps because they are free and available to us every day. Because they are offered daily at no cost, we are called to receive the gifts they were designed to provide.

Through the sacraments and prayer, God wants to calm the storm caused by body obsession. Living with this difficulty is like living in a violent storm, and probably at times feels like a hurricane, and therefore we need shelter. Our shelter is our Catholic Faith, and God is begging us to accept that faith.

And remember, if God says it is good, it's good.

CHAPTER 6

What Is Healthy?

For those who live according to the flesh set their minds on the things of the flesh, but those who live according to the Spirit set their minds on the things of the Spirit. To set the mind on the flesh is death, but to set the mind on the Spirit is life and peace.

—Romans 8:5–6

I have had countless male and female college students approach me over the years and inquire about achieving the perfect body. These people, in almost every case, already looked perfectly healthy. But what they wanted is to look *really* good. On one occasion, a young woman brought in a fitness magazine and showed me photos of fitness models she wanted to emulate. My comments were, "OK, I can give you a workout program and eating plan to get you to look like that. But you're not going to have any fun in life. You can't eat sugar or fatty foods anymore, so that means no dessert or fast food; you can't drink alcohol; and your workouts will need to be two to three hours per day, involving serious weight training and intense cardio sessions." Very quickly, her enthusiasm waned, and the topic of conversation changed to something far less intense.

In these instances, the students seemed to realize that something was wrong with this lifestyle. They are like most people in that they are drawn to beauty and nice body shape, but they want it at little cost. Perhaps they knew that such efforts would take away from other aspects of their life that are more important, such as their relationships, school, and work. Not to mention that such a life would be extreme and probably not worth it. Perhaps they really desire to lead a life of moderation which includes periodic rich foods and modest amounts of physical activity—something generally taught to students at a relatively young age these days. Is this wishful thinking? Maybe. Or perhaps they realize that the happiness they're seeking needs to come through different means altogether. The peace that God intends has nothing to do with today's magazine photographs, TV shows, and sexy movie scenes.

One of the recurring responsorial psalms at Mass is "The Lord is my light and my salvation. In whom should I be afraid?" (Ps 27). The beauty of this psalm is that it's not *really* a question but rather a statement, one of the basic tenets of Christianity. Recall that we discussed fear in the opening paragraph of the first chapter. There was brief dialogue regarding the question "What are you afraid of?" in which I discussed product manufacturer's dire attempt to persuade the public to buy their merchandise by using the age-old tactic of fear. That is, we are destined to fail in relationships, our jobs, et cetera unless we use a specific product. If that is true, however, then what is God's role in our lives? Is God something to contemplate at night only during our prayer time? Is God only to be worshipped on Sundays at Mass or does Psalm 27 have actual meaning?

The Mass is deep in Christ's messages, many of which are direct, and one of strongest messages addresses fear. During his passion, Christ experienced a great deal of fear himself, and thus knows this feeling well and is aware that we are anxious in our daily lives. A major fear, as discussed in chapter 1, is that we are worthless to society unless we are youthful and attractive. Christ's message is that we have dignity and worth regardless of our weight, shape, and degree of attractiveness. He desires a certain level of peace in our lives, and reminds us of that and encourages that peace through the Mass. Consider the following:

"The grace and peace of God our Father and the Lord Jesus Christ be with you all" (Greeting).

"Glory to God in the highest, and peace to his people on earth…" (Gloria).

"We offer them for your Holy Catholic Church, watch over it, Lord, and guide it; grant it peace and unity throughout the world" (Eucharistic Prayer).

"Deliver us, Lord, from every evil, and grant us peace in our day. In your mercy keep us free from sin and protect us from all anxiety as we wait in joyful hope for the coming of our Saviour, Jesus Christ" (following the Our Father).

"Peace I leave with you; my peace I give to you" (prior to the Sign of Peace).

"Now let us offer each other a Sign of Peace" (Sign of Peace).

"Go in peace, glorifying the Lord by your life" (one of the options as part of the Concluding Rite).

The number of times "peace" or "anxiety" are mentioned in the Mass begins to address how much God wants us to be free of anxiety. Being anxiety-free is what all Christians (and most everyone else for that matter) seek. We all desire peace because we know that it brings a certain degree of happiness—what many refer to as joy. However, most of us need help and even specific instructions to experience that harmony. This is the why the first of the theological virtues is Faith. It becomes clear to each one of us when we are relatively young that life is difficult, unfair, and even mean— some of which we experience directly as a result of body distortion. Faith is meant to address those feelings and bring us back to a good place, where we know that Christ's words resonate. Faith is trusting that something awaits us after this life and that there is something more than this imperfect body. Trusting in the grace of the sacraments allows God's grace to penetrate our heart and mind, and allows us to see that a perfect body is not a part of God's plan. Rather, God's plan is for us to use the body in perfect ways.

John Paul II said, "Victory . . . can and must take place in man's heart. This is the way to purity, that is to control one's own body in holiness and honor."[49] Victory, after all, is what we're after, isn't it? We don't want a poor body image or any other emotional issue to defeat us or to keep us from seeking the good. It's painful and frustrating when we allow TV shows and magazine photos to absorb us into a world where

---

[49]   TOB 2/4/81.

we think that curves and muscles in all the right places is where we will find true peace. The truth is, body distortion is very real and needs to be addressed.

Now let's address *our* role in this issue. An increase in faith, allowing the sacraments to be grace-filled, and any emotional healing that occurs will only come as a result of our participation in the process. Let's look at this another way. To conquer body distortion, our goal is to get over a big fence, and God is at the top of this fence reaching down with an outstretched arm. But we must climb to meet him. A poor body image was not created by chance or from nothing. We, at least to some extent, have contributed to the frustration and pain. *We* watched those racy TV programs and have seen countless images on the internet. *We* bought those magazines. And *we* have side-stepped or not embraced the grace that the sacraments offer.

If *impatience* was a virtue, we would all be saints. But a virtuous life includes a certain degree of patience and fortitude. Praying and striving for the good in all things takes discipline, as well as faith that living the Gospel will be rewarding. Note that Holy Mass is offered to us daily. If lifelong discipline was rewarded after receiving the Body of Christ one or two times, or all sin ceased after one confession, the offering of those sacraments would be rare, but that's not how it works. We must commit to our faith every day, and be on watch for all that might harm us. That's why St. Peter wrote, "Be sober, be watchful. Your adversary the devil prowls around *like* a roaring *lion*, seeking some one to devour" (1 Pt 5:8).

The "lion" in this case is the constant reminder from the media of how we *should* look. This is the media's plan: When ads appear of the perfect body, it pounces on our brain, and the image lingers and the inevitable occurs—we compare ourselves to the images and desire the product that will bring us a step closer to being the models in the ad. Few things are more powerful, and nothing seems to hold our soul prisoner more than images that make us feel bad about the body that God has given us.

These days most people are well aware of the rewards of healthy eating and exercise, especially as they relate to shaping the body. Various fitness-related magazines (twenty-five and counting), with those oh-so-appealing covers, TV shows, Internet images, commercials, and infomercials constantly remind us of how to do just about anything concerning body shape, fat loss, and muscle gain. A major theme of this book is that these images take us away from reality and cripple any chance at a developing a healthy body image. Therefore, a topic that should be addressed, at least concerning health and fitness, is weight and the percentage of body fat. Admittedly, there is some hesitation to discuss these issues to any degree since addressing this may be adding to the hysteria, not calming it. The fact remains that young adults as well as the general population can be anywhere on the spectrum of thin to morbidly obese and *still* suffer from body dissatisfaction. So let's address the weight and body fat topic since many who suffer from body distortion are sometimes so thin and/or muscular that a dose of reality is needed.

For a given height, body mass index (BMI) is proportional to weight, thus making it easy to calculate one's appropriate size. Even though it is considered flawed for a few reasons (e.g., if listed as "overweight," BMI cannot distinguish if the weight is excess fat or excess muscle), BMI is accepted as a legitimate means to determining healthy body weight, and it is comforting to the person in question since no touching occurs, and the only information needed is height and weight (see BMI chart and ratings).

A more precise and direct way to figure appropriate body composition is by testing the percent of body fat. Skin calipers, body-fat analyzers (e.g., Bod Pod), and underwater weighing are the most popular and valid methods to determine body fat (see percent body fat chart). As stated, it is unfortunate that despite many seeing that they are within the healthy ranges of BMI and body fat percent, anxiety over their bodies remains. That's where God's healing words come into play. Regardless of the amount of body fat we have, our dignity remains untouched. We are no less loved or any less dignified if we don't meet the standards of the latest magazine model, bodybuilder, or pro athlete.

It is vital that a distinction is made between being obsessed with and "taking care" of our bodies. All are aware that basic hygiene, modest amounts of exercise, and healthy eating should be attempted daily. Even the use of beauty products and keeping with fashion trends by itself does not signal any type of obsession, and is doubtful that it displeases God in any way. But it must also be noted that the failure to take care of the body is considered anywhere between disrespectful to God to sinful. Several books have been written that attempt to address these issues, such as *Does God Care How Much I Weigh?* and *Does God Care What I Eat?* The authors conclude, to no one's surprise, that God does indeed care about how we treat our bodies, and he expects that we will treat them with dignity.

Several popes throughout history have been strong supporters of physical health, and in particular were advocates of sport and physical activity, including Popes Pius XII (1939–1958) and John Paul II (1978–2005). Both spoke and wrote extensively about the role that physical activity plays in society as well as the role that morality and moderation play on the individual athlete.[50] Not surprisingly, the Vatican, under John Paul II, instituted the Office of Church and Sport that addresses the moral dimensions expected of athletes, as well as those who oversee sport. Among its purposes, this new office for the laity directs the athlete to see all forms of exercise as a means to develop the mind, soul, and body as God intended. Clearly, the Church encourages the human person to be physically active, but to always see it in the framework of Church teaching.[51] John Paul II said it well to a group of athletes:

> Athletic activity, in fact, highlights not only man's valuable physical abilities, but also his intellectual and spiritual capacities. It is not just physical strength and muscular efficiency, but it also has a soul and must show its complete face. This is why a true athlete must not let himself be carried away by an obsession with physical perfection, or be enslaved by the rigid laws of

---

[50] See Robert Feeney, *A Catholic Perspective: Physical Exercise and Sports*, Ignatius Press, 1995.

[51] CCC 2288, 2289.

production and consumption, or by purely utilitarian and hedonistic considerations.[52]

It's obvious that we should be conscious of any action that leads to an obsession or any negative view of the body, but we must also be careful when relying on fitness "experts," beauticians, surgeons, or any other professional on what it means to be fit or attractive, since some of them may be guilty of promoting obsessive behavior themselves. Following the standard guidelines of exercising can help us avoid this pitfall. For example, an aerobic workout of moderate intensity, for thirty to sixty minutes three to five days per week is staying within healthy parameters. Also encouraged by many fitness professionals is a modest weight training program, such as one to two sets per major muscle group each workout at two to three days per week.

We should consider our eating habits as well. Just as with exercise, there's an abundance of nutrition-based information to sift through. *What and when should I eat? What are the best foods to increase energy and boost metabolism?* Good questions indeed, but in-depth discussions of these and other concerns are addressed in other books. The basics of healthy eating, however, can be understood in the new "My Plate" which recently replaced the traditional food pyramid. While the "plate" is simplified, the concept can be grasped: Grains such as whole wheat bread, whole wheat pasta, and fiber-based breakfast cereal should dominate most meals. Additionally, considerable servings of vegetables, fruit, and

---

[52]   John Paul II, address to the international convention: "During the time of the Jubilee: The face and soul of sport," 9/28/00.

dairy products, and to a lesser degree, beans and lean meats should be a part of your daily intake of calories. Note that high (especially saturated) fat and high sugar-based products such as desserts and sweetened beverages are suggested in minimal amounts.[53]

Despite the general encouragement to lead a healthy life-style, keep in mind that even the strictest personal trainer would allow a day or two off per week, nor would he or she frown on the occasional fast food meal or bowl of ice cream. However, just as with our sacramental and prayer life, healthy behaviors need to be practiced with overwhelming regularity or any clear benefits would be doubtful. And just as was stated earlier that we participate in ways that harm our body image, we must accept responsibility that excess body fat and poor fitness levels did not magically appear. Healing can start when we admit that we have made choices along the way that directly lead to these poor health-related conditions. Habitual bad eating and lack of physical activity, which generally lead to a high BMI, play a direct part in poor body issues.[54] Conversely, the data has been consistent in correlating moderate and consistent exercise regimens[55]

53   For more details on the food pyramid, see http://www.mypyra-mid.gov/.

54   A. Weaver and E. Byers, "The relationships among body image, body mass index, exercise, and sexual functioning in heterosexual women," 2006, *Psychology of Women Quarterly, 30*, 333–39.

55   R. Henry, M. Anshel and T. Michael, "Effects of aerobic and cir-cuit training on fitness and body image among women," 2006, *Journal of Sport Behavior, 29*, 281–303; H. Hausenblas and E. Fallon, "Relationship among body image, exercise behavior and exercise dependence symptoms," 2002, *International Journal of Eating Disorders, 32*, 179–85.

and even one-bout sessions of light physical activity with a positive body image.[56]

It's problematic when exercise and diet behavior become extreme, in either direction. Alarms should sound when the desire to "achieve the better body" turns into getting absolutely "ripped" or believing that the thinner we are, the better our lives will be or even that true peace is attainable. On the other hand, a lack of effort in caring for the body is just as troubling. Furthermore, obsessing over the perfect body means we neither have the time nor care to meet the needs of others, and on the other hand, poor eating and exercise habits result in low energy levels or poor health that make it virtually impossible to serve others, even if there is a true desire to do so.

Are these concepts relatively easy to understand? Is it difficult for many to eat healthy and exercise regularly? Is it difficult to turn away from the images that elevate the awareness of our body's imperfections? Yes, all three times. But that's the purpose of this book and that's one of the reasons for Christ's birth, death, and resurrection. The central purpose of this book is to draw attention to the relationship between the coming of Christ and the intense feelings associated with a poor body distortion.

---

[56]   S. Scarpa, A. Nart, E. Gobbi and A. Carraro, "Does women's attitudinal state body image improve after one session of posture correction exercises?" 2011, *Social Behavior & Personality: An International Journal, 39*, 1045–52; S. Vocks, T. Hechler, S. Rohrig and T. Legenbauer, "Effects of a physical exercise session on state body image: The influence of pre-experimental body dissatisfaction and concerns about weight and shape," 2009, *Psychology & Health, 24*, 713–28.

So how do we gauge the severity of a poor body image? A poor body image, formerly known to researchers and psychologists as Body Dysmorphic Disorder, wasn't officially recognized as a psychological issue until 1997. And since it is a relatively new topic of study, professionals are still in the infant stage of finding meaningful solutions to this complex problem. Still, let's investigate whether you may need help beyond this book.

You may have body dysmorphic disorder if you:

- Constantly compare your appearance with others.
- Refuse to let your picture be taken, or are extremely self-conscious in photos.
- Keep checking a certain body part that you think is flawed (e.g., your nose or belly) and measure the flaw frequently.
- Make drastic attempts to hide your flaws.
- Feel anxious and self-conscious around other people.
- Avoid leaving the house unless you absolutely have to (since body dysmorphic disorder has been known to limit your social interaction and romantic relationships).
- Refer to yourself in demeaning ways such as "hideous," "ugly," and "disgusting."
- Seek or strongly consider cosmetic surgery to look perfect: liposuction, rhinoplasty, etc.

By responding in the affirmative to one or more of the above, one may feel that a degree of body disorder exists, thus prompting some form of psychological treatment. While a more aggressive form of therapy may be needed to repair this issue for some, there should be no definitive decisions based on the questions or information provided here. Keep in mind the intention of this book. Still, let's investigate this further and consider the following questions:

Have you admitted to yourself that you may struggle with body dysmorphic disorder?

This is where the saying "The truth can set you free" comes in. Simply put, healing body image problems starts with honesty and acceptance.

Will talking to your close friends and trusted family members help?

Attempt to explain how you feel about your body. Be open to healing your body image problems or body dysmorphic disorder through experiencing God's love through others.

Do you treat yourself well?

Committing to a healthy lifestyle that includes eating right and exercising regularly can calm a great deal of the anxieties that accompany a poor body image.

Can you direct your thoughts and actions to something else when negative thoughts of your body appear?

For example, ridding yourself of conversations about beauty, fashion/muscle magazines, and physically appealing TV shows. And a follow-up question may be…

Can you commit to embracing the theme of Theology of the Body and Scripture as it addresses the body?

The full intention of this book is to use the Word of God and St. John Paul II's Theology of the Body to transform our thoughts so we see our body as a gift, regardless of our body fat percent, level of attractiveness, height, and various bodily imperfections.

Being honest with ourselves, with those around us, and in the confessional is not easy. But being true to ourselves places us on the road to lower anxiety and closer to God. Developing an obsession with our bodies harms John Paul II's central theme of Theology of the Body—that an appropriate use of the body is at the core of God's divine plan. The great pope set out to change the way we see our bodies and makes it clear that our primary task in life is to experience the love of God and share the language of God's love with others. While this book may not completely heal body distortion, it is this book's purpose to expose this issue and offer two of the most powerful healing tools that our faith offers so we have a chance to mend it: Theology of the Body and the power of the sacraments.

And remember, if God says it is good, it's good.

CHAPTER 7

OK, My Body's Not Perfect, Now What?

I praise you, for I am wounderously made. Wonderful are you works! You know me right well.

—Psalm 139:14

In the years leading up to his death, it became known that Pope John Paul II was suffering from a degenerative condition. While medical experts agree Parkinson's disease took its toll on the pope, there was never an official diagnosis. Regardless, John Paul II brought a face to suffering. Through it all, he continued to write, celebrate Mass, and make public appearances until he was simply too ill to travel. Even then, his final days were marked with appearances and brief messages from his window at the Vatican. But as many recall, in the final stage of his papacy, the reports of his addresses were riddled with comments about his posture, slurred speech, drool, and evident shaking, as much as it was about his message. Despite his ailments, the pope continued to fulfill his purpose. He was called as a priest to serve the people of God, and eventually as pope he was called to lead the Church. He never gave up, and he never gave in.

Considered handsome, athletic, and a talented drama enthusiast in his younger days, he refused to let his ego get the better of him. Until his death, he continued his tiring schedule in spite of his frailty and increasing illness. This alone illustrates the greatness of John Paul II. He understood and lived out the notion that a person's dignity is not tied to beauty, fame, or a legacy. In short, he fully recognized God's call to love others despite of his physical shortcomings.

The pope demonstrated so much integrity and humility in his failing health that most people, even non-Catholics, began respecting him more deeply than before. In our weakness, too many of us would probably do the opposite when faced with a similar situation. In fact, we have seen in our society that in a few instances, especially people who feel the need to protect an image (actors, politicians, etc.), surround themselves with advisors or family members who will go to great lengths to ensure that the public remembers their loved one in a more youthful, healthy, and vibrant state.

John Paul II was not concerned with preserving his reputation as the once-youthful and energetic leader of the Catholic Church. Humility, that ever-elusive trait, was something he may have mastered long before his old age. In fact, he had probably practiced it for decades, giving credibility to the belief that we become virtuous with practice. But most of us are simply not that righteous, and we probably discovered early in life that pride and selfish behavior are an integral part of the human experience and governs almost every move we make. Moreover, ego-based sins are particularly troubling to those who are well catechized or well-read in Scripture, since there is a higher level of self-awareness and perhaps a stronger level of expectation, and thus remorse. But this awareness should not be looked at as a burden. On the contrary, we want to accept this awareness as a gift and seek out the sacraments to guide us to the healing we need.

As human beings, we have limitations. These limitations involve every aspect of our physical existence. We will age, our skin will wrinkle and sag, and if it hasn't already, our hair will fall out. In addition, our response to exercise and healthy eating is not always enthusiastic. This tells us that our bodies are not perfect.

John Paul II noted in his Theology of the Body talks that before original sin, the body and soul were harmonious, and no conflict involving the greatness or purpose of the body existed. In addition, the ability to choose good and dismiss evil was simple and natural. The Fall, however, produced a division between the body and soul, thus threatening the unity of the person and ultimately creating a threat in our relationship with God.[57] Still, God-given freedom allows us to choose the good in everything. In the case of body image, we have the choice, daily, to accept the gift or obsess over it in its imperfections.

As part of our freedom, we can choose to watch raunchy music videos or reality shows, look at fashion magazines, and engage in conversations that are critical about our bodies, all of which play a role in devaluing the body and chip away at

---

[57]   TB 5/28/80.

the positive body image that exists. In actuality, those TV shows and magazines are generally not concerned about our body image; they are trying to make money off us. Therefore, our responsibilities must include promoting the good within ourselves, and that in turn would lead to the common good in society. Participating in matters that add to our (or others) poor body image means we are culpable, at least to a degree. Seeking our own salvation, and playing a role in the salvation of others, is quite a responsibility. But that road to salvation is scattered with assistance through Scripture, the *Catechism*, and the writings of the faithful.[58]

Our faith is designed to help us to acquire wisdom. And we need to rely on that wisdom so we can, for instance, recognize the difference between healthy habits and obsessive behaviors that are most often triggered by magazines or the variety of images on TV and the internet. Further, these triggers may be magnified when we are in the presence of others, especially those in which we are seeking approval. By early adulthood, it becomes obvious our thoughts and actions are greatly determined by our circle of friends. So, to assist in our efforts to create healthier relationships, ponder this saying from St. Francis de Sales: "Love everyone with a great love, but have no friendship except for those that communicate with you in the things of virtue." This saying should help explain why your parents were so concerned with those you "hung out" with when you were younger.

As children, and even in adolescence, we can expect our parents to be held accountable for *our* actions, at least in

---

[58]   CCC 1913, 1914, 1917.

part. But as we get older, we must have an awareness that seemingly innocent actions can lead to obsessive or harmful behavior. It is also vital to distinguish between a good habit and an addiction when there is a disproportionate amount of time, money, and effort vying for perfection rather than meeting our basic spiritual and emotional needs and the needs of those around us. A good question to ask ourselves may be: "Do my thoughts and actions involving my eating, exercise, and other leisure activities draw me closer to or further away from God?"

Referring to God, St. Augustine said, "Our hearts are restless until they rest in you." Society, for a variety of reasons, suggests our hearts rest in material things, beauty, and sexiness. But as people of God, we know better. Regardless of the time in history, distractions from God have always existed, and today distractions are literally in the palm of our hand. Resting our hopes, dreams, and faith in anything other than God will lead us to a life of frequent letdowns and even complete misery. Christ came to show us a new way. His way, radical to most in his time as well as the present, is the only hope in a world driven by the need to obtain a small waist size, the constant desire to be good-looking, calorie-counting, and trying to be the sexiest one in the room. To combat against all of this, God sent his only Son, gave him a body like you and me, and told us to listen to him (Lk 9:35).

There's an old Roman adage: *Live the life that you believe, rather than believe the life you live.* This profound statement can be directly applied to body image because our culture is extremely successful in telling us how to live. Even though many of us have received enough instruction on the faith and enough grace to lead a Christian life, the world is complicated and can be relentless on our spirit; it can even be downright evil at times. Shallow conversations, magazines, soap operas, and select TV programs can skew what is good or common. In fact, some reality shows could not be further from reality. Take, for instance, a show like *The Bachelor*, with a concept that includes twenty single, young women living in the same house vying for the attention of *one* man. What's real about that? Further, and more importantly, to what extent do shows like this harm us?

Dr. Nora Volkow, a well-known addiction specialist, has focused her research on how the brain creates and responds to dopamine. Dopamine, a neurotransmitter commonly associated with pleasure, also plays a key role in the addiction process. It has become clear to Volkow that there is a relationship between our behaviors and addiction. She gained insight on this concept when she showed various photographs to cocaine addicts. When the addicts were shown innocent images such as a stream or a child's toy, their brains had no reaction chemically. However, when they were shown a photo of someone snorting cocaine, dopamine was released. And the higher the amount of dopamine released, the more they wanted the drug.

So, what does an addiction to drugs have to do with body image, and in particular, seeing youthful, beautiful faces and bodies? Well, maybe everything. Images of perfect bodies are everywhere and perhaps some of us are addicted to these images. Just as some live through the pages of a romance novel, we may live through the photos of picture-perfect bodies. Many of us are probably guilty of the daydream where our lives are so much better when we are given a great body or a perfect face. Due to the instant pleasure that this daydream may bring, we play it again and again so that it becomes an obsession. An obsession, by its definition, mirrors an addiction, and therein lays the problem.

Certain TV shows, movies, and glossy magazine photos have captivated us and have taken our minds and souls hostage. Unless we seriously limit or omit this from our daily lives, we will begin to think that what we see is indeed reality, and worse, normal or even healthy. Consider what former supermodel Cindy Crawford once said: "In the morning, *I* don't even look like Cindy Crawford," strongly suggesting that even she needs a lot of help to look "perfect." In addition, Crawford has admitted to numerous cosmetic surgery procedures, many while she was in her modeling prime.

Watching particular programs and reading fashion magazines usually means we are searching for something, perhaps, as we may tell ourselves, for a simple form of entertainment. But at the nucleus, what we often see is sinister because it hooks us and plays on our vulnerabilities—which are our imperfections. What's awful is that many of these outlets are outrageously popular and are too easily accessed. As a result, too many succumb to an obsession. Trying to be perfect takes an emotional toll since perfection can never be attained. Excessive tattoos, extreme or numerous body piercings, and the normalcy of cosmetic surgery all convey that there's a great deal of unhappiness with the body God gave us. It seems that many are looking for something more or something better for satisfaction to occur. I once heard a woman, who was *already* covered in tattoos, say, "I'm still looking for the perfect tattoo." It's obvious that she is looking for something, but something that probably has little to do with the ink on her skin.

But what *are* we looking for, anyway? Whatever it is, our mortality must be accepted at some point. Even if bodily perfection were granted, true peace would still evade us, since true peace is when we are in full communion with God, and being in full communion means that we must embrace everything God offers us, especially our bodies. The sooner we can adopt this truth, the sooner we can shed a life of anxiety and pain associated with body obsession. God's wish is for us to avoid searching for anything that widens the gap between us and him. He desires, as we do, for us to be free of pain, disappointment, and emptiness.

Because of our struggles, God sent his Son to teach us about being "born again" so that we leave the old ways behind and start life anew (Jn 3:3). In other words, Christ calls us to experience a conversion. The risen Christ provides the courage to live that new life, and each day we are commanded to reclaim ourselves to God and to accept righteousness, not sin (Rom 6:1–23). When Christ died, he took all sins with him—all that occurred before and after his crucifixion. *This* is why the crucifix is so common in our churches, and *this* is why Good Friday is so powerful.

If we choose to carry our burdens, and disallow Christ to do what he promised, the love of God cannot penetrate our soul, nor can we know what God wants for us. The healing of body obsession begins when we firmly acknowledge that the pursuit of perfection is fruitless and that it seriously harms our spirit to keep us from living in God's grace. Bear in mind, however, that a transformation does not mean that injustice and dark moments won't occur,[59] but it does mean that we won't walk through these times alone.

It is impossible to determine the single best way to improve body image, but two things are clear. One, practical tactics must be in place, such as watching less TV, being more selective about the magazines we browse, and choosing our friends wisely. Two, God needs to play a substantial role. If anything is evident to those with faith, it's the frailty of the human person, thus the powerful biblical theme and fundamental need of a consistent and sincere relationship with God. God provides purpose, and most importantly with the issue of a poor body image always looming, we need to turn many of our thoughts to using our body to communicate with him. Prayer and the sacraments give us grace. And grace can give us that discipline to avoid the triggers that lead us to thinking our body is worthless. Even better, grace can provide the insight and the inner peace to see our bodies as a tool to bring us closer to our creator.

Another underlying reason to overcome this battle within ourselves is that we want to avoid passing on body obsession to our children. A common, yet overwhelming, feeling that many of us experience when we first look into the eyes of our newborn is the desire to protect them at all costs. While physical protection is part of it, this should also extend to protecting their soul. This is why, among faithful Christians, there is a lot of discussion about homeschooling and limiting TV and Internet access—ideals that are often dismissed

---

[59]   CCC 164.

by casual onlookers as radical or even militant. But once we start having babies, such actions, as they should, usually make more sense. We cannot change the world, but we can certainly make serious and distinct efforts to incubate, at least to a degree, the world in which our children live.

From the day of our confirmation, we became deeply embedded in Christ and should rely on the gifts of the Holy Spirit, gifts like strength and wisdom to guide us to healing and conversion.[60] Although we know the importance of turning to God, the allure of trying to be physically perfect is very powerful, and there's an ongoing battle within us about it. This is why God asks us to start fighting and to never give up. Persevering in the good will bring the greatest reward known to man: to see the face of God.

And remember, if God says it is good, it's good.

---

[60]   CCC 1316, 1433, 1831.

PART II

Welcome to Part II!

Hopefully you were able to read part I, but if not, that's okay. These activities, which can be done in a group or through private reflection, are not dependent on having read the first part. Simply dive into the first one and get going.

But if you have jumped straight here, it's recommended to return to part I later and give it a good read to ensure you get the full benefit of this book.

Group Structure and Timing

If you're doing this part in a group setting, it's recommended that you spend roughly ten minutes on each activity. If you take a five-minute break in the middle, that's about a two-hour event. If that's too long, feel free to skip around and only do a portion of the activities, or spend more time on some than others. This is meant to be flexible. The two-hour structure is only a recommendation.

The recommended group size is five to fifteen, but less or more can work. For larger groups, consider breaking into small groups for each activity (and rotate members). If possible, split the groups up by gender, with a male adult leading the males, and a female adult leading the females.

It's assumed most groups will consist of young people, though adults can suffer from body image issues too and may benefit from a group setting and discussion. If you have a younger group, try to pair them in similar age brackets. No one under fourteen should engage in the activities considering the topic at hand.

Group Facilitator?

If you are a group facilitator, the first thing you'll want to do is scan the activities ahead of time. If you plan to make the group event shorter or jump around and skip certain activities, you'll need to know which ones you want to do and which ones you want to skip. In other words, you'll want to have your own plan in place. You'll also want to review the activities beforehand to ensure you have all the materials you need (some can be done with nothing, but others require certain things) as well as to review the questions. While there is no answer key since answers will vary with each participant, you'll want to take down some notes on how you might foster group discussion with each one. This way when discussion runs dry, you'll have something to refer to and be better able to get things going.

If you are leading a group of younger people, remember to be sensitive about this content. Young people can truly struggle with issues of body image, reputation, peer pressure, and self worth. These activities are meant to help not just through the education it provides but *through the powerful technique of hearing their peers open up and discuss the same things they are going through.* That being said, don't force anyone to participate in group discussion. Take things as they come. Try to keep the pace of the session on track, but if fruitful discussion opens up, don't be afraid to let it continue. They can always finish the activities at home.

While the session is meant to be a one-time thing, consider scheduling a follow-up session some months later to see if anyone wants to share positive changes they have experienced.

Finally, thank you for taking the time to shepherd young people through this sensitive but important topic that plagues so many in our society today.

Positive and Negative Body Image

What is body image?
It's quite possible you've heard about body image before and even understand it on a basic level. Perhaps you read the first part of this book and know a lot about it now. But in case you jumped straight to the activities or are doing these activities first, here's a quick rundown.

Body image is simply how we view our physical self. This includes every part of you (your face, hands, feet, arms, legs, etc.). What makes it interesting (and complicated) is that body image can be affected by many things. For example, body image can be determined by how we dress, if we exercised that day, looking at photos of models, comments made by others about how we look, if we are an athlete, or simply if we are in a good mood that day. Like I said, it's complicated.

Let's take a look at some of the basics and discuss positive and negative body image.

1. What are the characteristics of a positive body image? Here's what a young person would probably say if they had a positive body image:

- "I am comfortable with the body and face that God has given me."

96

- "I appreciate and understand that there are people of naturally different body sizes and shapes."
- "I know that a person's body shape and size have nothing to do with their dignity and value and the love that God has for them."
- "I refuse to spend excessive time on: exercise, making exact calorie counts on meals, and selecting the 'perfect' outfit."

Now you list three other comments a person with a positive body image might say:

_____

_____

_____

2. Place a check by each of the comments in no. 1 that you have thought yourself.

3. What are the characteristics of a poor body image?
Here's what a young person would probably say if they had a negative body image:

- "People tell me I am pretty, but I don't think so."
- "I refuse to believe that people have naturally different body sizes and shapes."
- "A person's body shape and size has something to do with their value in society and the love that God has for them."

- "I constantly feel awkwardness and shame because of my physical appearance."

Now you list three other comments a person with a negative body image might say:

_____

_____

_____

4. Place a check by each of the comments in no. 3 that you have thought yourself.

5. Considering your responses to this opening activity, do you have an overall positive or negative body image? Explain why.

_____

_____

_____

_____

_____

_____

_____

The Catechism and Body Image

The teaching of the Catholic Church is summarized in a book called the *Catechism of the Catholic Church*. It discusses just about everything you can think of regarding our faith, morality, and everyday challenges. While the *Catechism* does not discuss body image directly, it does encourage us to apply our Catholic faith to everyday challenges, which would include the way we see our bodies. So let's take a moment to look at some specifics from our *Catechism*.

Read these passages either to yourself or aloud if you're with a group:

> The human body shares in the dignity of "the image of God": it is a human body precisely because it is animated by a spiritual soul, and it is the whole human person that is intended to become, in the body of Christ, a temple of the Spirit:
>
> "Man, though made of body and soul, is a unity. Through his very bodily condition he sums up in himself the elements of the material world. Through him they are thus brought to their highest perfection and can raise their voice in praise freely given to the Creator. For this reason man may not despise his bodily

life. Rather he is obliged to regard his body as good and to hold it in honor since God has created it and will raise it up on the last day."

The unity of soul and body is so profound that one has to consider the soul to be the "form" of the body: i.e., it is because of its spiritual soul that the body made of matter becomes a living, human body; spirit and matter, in man, are not two natures united, but rather their union forms a single nature. (CCC 364–65)

1. What are your initial thoughts after reading these passages from the *Catechism*?

_____

_____

_____

_____

2. How do these readings relate to body image?

_____

_____

_____

_____

3. God could have made us only spiritual beings. Why do you think he gave us a body?

_____

_____

_____

_____

_____

4. Explain the relationship between a positive body image and these words from the *Catechism*.

_____

_____

_____

_____

_____

The Book of Genesis: Where Body Image Began

The Book of Genesis is one of the most familiar books of the Bible. There are several reasons for this.

First, and perhaps most importantly, there is the story of how God created all things, including human beings. The famous story of Adam and Eve is interesting, but it also chronicles the origin of sin as it relates to us as physical beings.

Second, while the Book of Genesis tells a number of stories, with a focus on the first inhabitants of the world, the meaning of our lives is spelled out in many ways. Let's take a look at how the Book of Creation relates to our topic at hand; that is, how we view our bodies.

Before discussing the next few questions, please read Genesis 1:26–31, copied here for your convenience.

> Then God said, "Let us make man in our image, after our likeness; and let them have dominion over the fish of the sea, and over the birds of the air, and over the cattle, and over all the earth, and over every creeping thing that creeps upon the earth." So God created man

in his own image, in the image of God he created him; male and female he created them. And God blessed them, and God said to them, "Be fruitful and multiply, and fill the earth and subdue it; and have dominion over the fish of the sea and over the birds of the air and over every living thing that moves upon the earth." And God said, "Behold, I have given you every plant yielding seed which is upon the face of all the earth, and every tree with seed in its fruit; you shall have them for food. And to every beast of the earth, and to every bird of the air, and to everything that creeps on the earth, everything that has the breath of life, I have given every green plant for food." And it was so. And God saw everything that he had made, and behold, it was very good. And there was evening and there was morning, a sixth day.

1. When God declared that all of his creations are "good," what did he mean when referring to the body?

_____

_____

_____

_____

_____

2. List three reasons why man is the greatest of all of God's creations?

_____

_____

_____

_____

_____

3. Why would it make God sad if you thought his creation—the body—is *not* good?

_____

_____

_____

_____

_____

Now read Genesis 3:1–7 about the Fall of Man:

> Now the serpent was more subtle than any other wild creature that the Lord God had made. He said to the woman, "Did God say, 'You shall not eat of any tree of the garden'?" And the woman said to the serpent, "We may eat of the fruit of the trees of the garden; but God said, 'You shall not eat of the fruit of the tree which

is in the midst of the garden, neither shall you touch it, lest you die.'" But the serpent said to the woman, "You will not die. For God knows that when you eat of it your eyes will be opened, and you will be like God, knowing good and evil." So when the woman saw that the tree was good for food, and that it was a delight to the eyes, and that the tree was to be desired to make one wise, she took of its fruit and ate; and she also gave some to her husband, and he ate. Then the eyes of both were opened, and they knew that they were naked; and they sewed fig leaves together and made themselves aprons.

4. What is the relationship between these words of Genesis and how we view our bodies? Do we listen to others to tell us our value? Why is it a problem if we did listen to others about how our bodies should look?

_____

_____

_____

_____

_____

5. Discuss how these meditations have made you view the Book of Genesis in a different way, or your own body image in a different way.

_____

_____

_____

_____

_____

Body Image Survey

This is not an official survey that can legitimately determine whether someone has a negative or positive body image. But it can give you an idea of where you are with this issue.

Answer the questions by picking the response that best fits for you. At the end, add up your points (Strongly Disagree is worth 1 each time, Disagree 2, etc.).

1.) My main reason/motivation to exercise and eat better is to look good, rather than to be healthy.

(1) Strongly Disagree	(2) Disagree	(3) Neutral	(4) Agree	(5) Strongly Agree

2.) I have had feelings of wanting to look better after looking at photos of people my age.

(1) Strongly Disagree	(2) Disagree	(3) Neutral	(4) Agree	(5) Strongly Agree

3.) I often have feelings of wanting to look like other people in my social circles.

(1) Strongly Disagree	(2) Disagree	(3) Neutral	(4) Agree	(5) Strongly Agree

4.) Overall, I do not like the way I look.

(1) Strongly Disagree	(2) Disagree	(3) Neutral	(4) Agree	(5) Strongly Agree

5.) I am very sensitive if my peers were to make negative comments about my physical appearance.

(1) Strongly Disagree	(2) Disagree	(3) Neutral	(4) Agree	(5) Strongly Agree

6.) I avoid social situations, in part, because of my negative body image.

(1) Strongly Disagree	(2) Disagree	(3) Neutral	(4) Agree	(5) Strongly Agree

7.) I often choose clothes that are most "flattering" to my body shape/size.

(1) Strongly Disagree	(2) Disagree	(3) Neutral	(4) Agree	(5) Strongly Agree

8.) I often think about the parts of my body that need "improvement."

(1) Strongly Disagree	(2) Disagree	(3) Neutral	(4) Agree	(5) Strongly Agree

9.) People who are thin/low percent body fat are always attractive.

(1) Strongly Disagree	(2) Disagree	(3) Neutral	(4) Agree	(5) Strongly Agree

10.) I have changed something about myself after seeing something on TV or the Internet.

(1) Strongly Disagree	(2) Disagree	(3) Neutral	(4) Agree	(5) Strongly Agree

Add up your points to see where you fall:

- 10–20 points: You suffer from very little to no body image issues.

- 21–30 points: You may have a slight problem with your body image but nothing severe.
- 31–40 points: Your body image is a large part of your life and something you worry about more than the average person.
- 41–50 points: You have an issue with your body image to such a degree that it essentially dominates your life.

Again, this survey is not official. But most people probably fall in that 20–30 point range. It's natural to care about how you look and what others think of you, but when we take this to the extreme, there's a problem.

Let's take a look at some of the survey questions in more depth so we can ask some important questions.

1. Considering *My main reason/motivation to exercise and eat better is to look good, rather than to be healthy.* Regardless of your response to this, provide three reasons why God might be happy that you exercised regularly?

_____

_____

_____

_____

_____

2. Considering *I often choose clothes that are most "flattering" to my body shape/size.* What do you think God would say to you about presenting yourself in a more "flattering" way?

_____

_____

_____

_____

_____

3. In looking at no. 1, do you think your parents would have similar reasons as God would for being happy that you wanted to exercise? For no. 2, what do you think your parents would say about trying to flatter others?

_____

_____

_____

_____

_____

4. Considering *I often think about the parts of my body that need improvement.* If you were to make the request directly to God to improve specific parts of your body, what do you think he would say to you? Be specific.

_____

_____

_____

_____

_____

The Power of Photoshop: Part I

Materials needed:

- A fashion magazine (preferably one each for men and women) or multiple, depending on the size of the group.
- Sticky notes cut four to five times to create tabs.
- Pen or pencil.

The following story is pulled from chapter 4. Feel free to re-read it as a refresher even if you have already read the first part of the book.

A couple of years ago, when I created and taught the course "Weight Loss, Weight Gain and Body Image," I spent a lot of time scheduling guest speakers for the class. Some of the speakers included a plastic surgeon, a gastric bypass surgery nurse, a registered dietitian for obese clients, and an editor for a women's magazine. This magazine editor spoke to my class on the first session. She talked to the students about Photoshop, a common software program that most magazine editors use to manipulate just about everything found in a photo. For instance, they can remove a tree from a picnic scene, make a dress a brighter shade of red, or make the model look "better." Her talk to my class, at my urging, focused on the latter.

She discussed in detail how editors, including herself, use this basic computer software to whiten teeth, remove veins from the white of the eye, improve imperfect skin, add muscle to a man, and decrease fat on a woman. She showed specific changes she made in the photos of her own magazine, as well as other (mainly fashion) magazines. She stated that, while models are naturally attractive, none—at least in the way they appear in magazines—are as perfect as they seem. Her point was that the very models that the readers are desperately aspiring to emulate don't even exist.

The class, made up of traditional age college students (eighteen to twenty-two), was silent with awe throughout her presentation. I am sure the students had thoughts of everything from "She can't be serious" to "How long have we been duped?" But after a few more comments from the editor on this subject, one of the female students, in near tears, said, "Why do they do that to us?"

With that, I almost cried myself.

1. What are your immediate thoughts about this story?

_____

_____

_____

_____

_____

2. Are you like the student in the story and find yourself angry or frustrated when looking at such magazines? Or do you simply find yourself appreciating (and perhaps feeling envious) of the overwhelming perfection and beauty found in magazine photos? Explain.

_____

_____

_____

_____

_____

Using your fashion magazine, tab or mark the following:

- Unnaturally white eyes (remember if you get close to someone's eyes you see red vessels, but Photoshop whites them out).
- Thin (and perhaps) unrealistic models.
- Models who seem to be having a great time/enjoying life.
- Revealing clothing (and the differences in clothing between male and female).

3. How many of the pages that you marked depict realistic body proportions? How many depict unrealistic body proportions?

4. How many advertisements did you see of people who seem to be enjoying life? Of these, how realistic is the ad in suggesting that this product could deliver that corresponding level of joy the models seem to be experiencing?

_____

_____

_____

_____

5. Make a list of the common physical characteristics of the women in the magazine. In other words, what about these women is similar? How do they differ?

_____

_____

_____

_____

6. Make a list of the common physical characteristics of the men. How are all the men similar? How do they differ?

_____

_____

_____

_____

The Power of Photoshop: Part II

To begin this activity, read Romans 6:12–16:

> Let not sin therefore reign in your mortal bodies, to make you obey their passions. Do not yield your members to sin as instruments of wickedness, but yield yourselves to God as men who have been brought from death to life, and your members to God as instruments of righteousness. For sin will have no dominion over you, since you are not under law but under grace. What then? Are we to sin because we are not under law but under grace? By no means! Do you not know that if you yield yourselves to any one as obedient slaves, you are slaves of the one whom you obey, either of sin, which leads to death, or of obedience, which leads to righteousness?

1. What are your immediate thoughts on these words from Paul in relation to the magazine task from activity 5 you just completed? How does the practice of Photoshop seem sinful and make our bodies "instruments of wickedness"? How might we become like "obedient slaves" to something like Photoshop?

_____

_____

_____

_____

_____

2. What type of judgment would Paul make on these magazine photos you addressed in activity 5?

_____

_____

_____

_____

_____

Now read 2 Corinthians 5:16–17:

> From now on, therefore, we regard no one from a
> human point of view; even though we once regarded

Christ from a human point of view, we regard him thus no longer. Therefore, if any one is in Christ, he is a new creation; the old has passed away, behold, the new has come.

3. How do you think these verses could relate to body image in general? What is meant by a "new creation" and the "old" passing away?

_____

_____

_____

_____

_____

4. Did reading the Bible give you a better and healthier perspective on the issue of body image? What questions still linger?

_____

_____

_____

_____

_____

Activity 7

We're Just Different

You've probably heard that no two snowflakes are alike. But they look similar, don't they? You also may know that human fingerprints, although seemingly identical, are not the same either.

Our faces and bodies are kind of like snowflakes and fingerprints. Think about the following: Two females can have the exact color blonde hair and blue eyes, yet look nothing alike. Two males can stand exactly 5'10" and each weigh 167 pounds, but would never be mistaken to be twins or even look-alikes.

What makes us human, in part, is that we all have similar body parts: hands, shoulders, legs, a face with two eyes, one mouth and nose, etc. We share these physical traits, yet this doesn't mean we look alike.

Due to everyday images, such as those of popular actors and actresses and photos in magazines and online, our tendency may be to think that everyone could, or worse, *should* look alike. However, natural differences in color of skin, eyes, and hair, along with a range of height and weight makes for a near-endless variety of combinations, meaning people can look similar but rarely identical.

Questions to consider regarding the commentary from above:

1. In general, what physical characteristics or traits are similar from country to country and around the world?

_____

_____

_____

_____

2. In general, what physical characteristics or traits are different from country to country and around the world?

_____

_____

_____

_____

3. How would the world change if everyone looked the same? That is, why should a variety of physical traits be viewed as a positive thing or at least accepted?

_____

_____

_____

_____

4. Make a list of physical traits that you can change about yourself. In other words, traits that you can do something about.

_____

_____

_____

_____

_____

_____

5. Make a list of physical traits that you cannot change about yourself.

_____

_____

_____

_____

_____

_____

6. Referring to the first list (things you can change), select the first three that you wrote down and consider what God would say to you if you asked his permission to change each. In other words, does God care about the change?

Word or phrase from the first list followed by God's thoughts:

1._____

_____

_____

2._____

_____

_____

3._____

_____

_____

Activity 8

Sticks and Stones

"Sticks and stones can break my bones, but words can never hurt me."

It's pretty safe to say that we have all heard this statement before. It's a saying that kids use as a "comeback" when someone is trying to verbally insult them. But when it comes to who we are physically, words can indeed be very hurtful—to our minds and to our souls.

Consider this true story about a ninth-grade girl who everyday took the school bus with the same students: One day, two of her male classmates simply blurted out, "Us guys agreed that you would be the prettiest girl in the class if you weren't fat." She was shocked by the comment but also by the unapologetic style in which they said it. Either way, she never forgot that day or those harmful words. And what was probably most surprising is that she wasn't fat or obese.

1. Does this story seem silly or exaggerated to you? Or does it seem real? Explain why. Have you ever overheard anything like this?

_____

_____

_____

_____

2. What has been said about *you* that hurt your feelings? Which comments were specifically about your face or body?

_____

_____

_____

_____

Read 2 Corinthians 12:9–10:

> But he said to me, "My grace is sufficient for you, for my power is made perfect in weakness." I will all the more gladly boast of my weaknesses, that the power of Christ may rest upon me. For the sake of Christ, then, I am content with weaknesses, insults, hardships, persecutions, and calamities; for when I am weak, then I am strong.

3. Considering your response to no. 2, how can these words of St. Paul bring you peace? In particular, how can weakness bring strength?

_____

_____

_____

_____

Read Proverbs 27:2:

> Let another praise you, and not your own mouth;
> a stranger, and not your own lips.

Now read Romans 12:3:

> For by the grace given to me I bid every one among you not to think of himself more highly than he ought to think, but to think with sober judgment, each according to the measure of faith which God has assigned him.

4. What do these verses say to you when you are given a compliment about how you look?

_____

_____

_____

_____

ACTIVITY 9

Body "Art"

A young woman, already covered in tattoos on both arms from her shoulders to her wrists, along with several others on her back, was overheard saying, "I'm still searching for the perfect tattoo."

Tattoos and piercings are not new or limited to the United States. In fact, in cultures much older than America, such "body art" goes back centuries and conveys many different and meaningful things, such as the importance that person has in their village or that they are available for marriage and trying to attract a mate.

In considering our own culture, just a few decades ago a large number of tattoos and multiple piercings would have been unexpected, even shocking or inappropriate to some. While most people are still uninterested in body art, tattoos and piercings have become more of the norm, regardless of age, sex, and social status.

Let's take a look at your feelings and thoughts on this topic.

1. To start, what is your first impression when you see a tattoo?

_____

_____

_____

_____

2. Refer to the opening statement above about the young woman. Discuss what you think she meant by her statement. What does it say about her habit of body art that she had so much of it and yet still hadn't found what she was looking for?

_____

_____

_____

_____

Read Leviticus 19:28 and Galatians 5:17:

> You shall not make any cuttings in your flesh on account of the dead or tattoo any marks upon you: I am the Lord. (Lv 19:28)

> For the desires of the flesh are against the Spirit, and the desires of the Spirit are against the flesh; for these are opposed to each other, to prevent you from doing what you would. (Gal 5:17)

Now read John 7:24 and 1 Samuel 16:7.

> Do not judge by appearances, but judge with right judgment. (Jn 7:24)

> But the LORD said to Samuel, "Do not look on his appearance or on the height of his stature, because I have rejected him; for the LORD sees not as man sees; man looks on the outward appearance, but the LORD looks on the heart." (Sm 16:7)

3. What do you think about these passages? How do they inform your conscience and opinions on "body art" and the wider issue of body image in general?

_____

_____

_____

_____

4. What would you say to someone who seeks your opinion on whether they should get a tattoo? Would you ever get one?

_____

_____

_____

_____

The Bible and the Body

Believe it or not, the Bible (both the Old and the New Testaments) has a lot to say about the human body. St. Paul, the writer of many books of the New Testament, is probably the most quoted on this subject. However, it is not only how often he speaks of the human body but what he says that's important. And like so many of these versus, written two thousand years ago or more, St. Paul writes about the human body in such a way that we can apply it to our world today. Let's take a look at some of what St. Paul says.

Read and reflect on 1 Corinthians 12:23–25:

> And those parts of the body which we think less honorable we invest with the greater honor, and our unpresentable parts are treated with greater modesty, which our more presentable parts do not require. But God has so adjusted the body, giving the greater honor to the inferior part, that there may be no discord in the body, but that the members may have the same care for one another.

1. Although St. Paul uses the body as a way to explain Christ's relationship to his followers, how would you view the body if these words were taken literally?

_____

_____

_____

_____

Read and reflect on 1 Corinthians 6:18–20:

> Shun immorality. Every other sin which a man commits is outside the body; but the immoral man sins against his own body. Do you not know that your body is a temple of the Holy Spirit within you, which you have from God? You are not your own; you were bought with a price. So glorify God in your body.

2. In these versus, St. Paul discusses the sinful uses of the body. Referring to the final sentence in verse 20, what are some ways that we could glorify God each day using our body?

_____

_____

_____

_____

Read and reflect on Galatians 5:13–18:

> For you were called to freedom, brethren; only do
> not use your freedom as an opportunity for the flesh,
> but through love be servants of one another. For the
> whole law is fulfilled in one word, "You shall love your
> neighbor as yourself." But if you bite and devour one
> another take heed that you are not consumed by one
> another.
>
> But I say, walk by the Spirit, and do not gratify
> the desires of the flesh. For the desires of the flesh
> are against the Spirit, and the desires of the Spirit are
> against the flesh; for these are opposed to each other,
> to prevent you from doing what you would. But if you
> are led by the Spirit you are not under the law.

3. What do you think St. Paul is saying about the spirit and
the flesh being directly opposed? How could developing a
greater appreciation for our own bodies show us that the
flesh and the spirit do not have to be opposed?

_____

_____

_____

_____

_____

Read and reflect on Romans 12:1–2:

I appeal to you therefore, brethren, by the mercies of God, to present your bodies as a living sacrifice, holy and acceptable to God, which is your spiritual worship. Do not be conformed to this world but be transformed by the renewal of your mind, that you may prove what is the will of God, what is good and acceptable and perfect.

4. What is St. Paul saying to the world today? How can these words help us grow closer to Christ?

_____

_____

_____

_____

_____

5. What are your overall thoughts of St. Paul's words? Which passages do you think will have long term impact on you and why?

_____

_____

_____

_____

_____

Physical Activity, Sports, and Body Image

Researchers set out to determine if playing sports and exercising, versus doing nothing at all, had an impact on high school boys and girls and how they viewed their bodies. The subjects were asked questions that identified them into one of two categories: aesthetic body image and functional body image. Aesthetic body image refers to those who focus on how "good" the body looks, which tends to encourage us to see our bodies from someone else's perspective. The bad news is placing a high priority on the aesthetic value has been known to cause shame, heightened anxiety, and lower body satisfaction. Functional body image, on the other hand, puts the focus on the physical capabilities and performance of a specific task, such as playing a sport, working out, or creating something like painting a picture or building a deck for someone's house.

Discuss the following questions. Afterwards, there is a short written piece that helps shape this discussion a little more.

1. For girls, what are some typical comments (compliments) from another person that would help someone form a positive aesthetic body image. List three.

_____

_____

_____

_____

_____

2. For boys, what are some typical comments (compliments) from another person that would help someone form a positive aesthetic body image. List three.

_____

_____

_____

_____

_____

3. In the opening paragraphs of this activity, we stated that playing a sport, working out, or creating something (like painting a picture or building a deck) could help us form a positive *functional* body image. List three tasks you do with some regularity that, with reflection, could help you appreciate the functional aspect of your body.

_____

_____

_____

_____

4. Now, list three tasks that directly allow us to help others in need. That is, what are the things you would *not* be able to do if you didn't have an able body?

_____

_____

_____

_____

_____

5. List specific things that you can do on a daily basis to shift your body image from aesthetic to functional.

_____

_____

_____

_____

_____

Feel free to read this section on your own at home or with the group.

The results of the research mentioned in the beginning of this activity showed that youth who play sports place a higher value on functional body image than those who exercise. This suggests that our experiences in sports are different from those in a formal exercise regimen (e.g., working out on a treadmill for thirty minutes). What this tells us about athletes is that when the objective is success in relation to a skill or outcome (e.g., winning the game), the participant tends to have a more positive view of their body. In other words, the athlete, in some way, reflects on the body as a means to accomplish something. Sometimes in sports settings this mindset is referred to as "the game is bigger than you," or "there's no 'I' in team."

Not surprisingly, researchers also found that those who engaged in regular exercise (treadmill workouts, cycling class, etc.) place a greater emphasis on the aesthetic qualities that others see (e.g., firmness of the arms, flat abs, shapely calf muscles). Placing value on how we look may develop or confirm that genuine worth is tied directly to physical beauty.

In summary, it's clear that those who choose to be active through exercise are doing it more to "look good," while those who play sports are more likely to be doing it for fun or for a higher cause. This doesn't mean exercise is wrong—of course it's important to remain healthy—but we are only fooling ourselves if we think exercise isn't mostly about impressing others with our looks (at least with young people and young adults).

Placing a high value on how we look is a choice. While having more toned muscles and less body fat is the outcome of an active lifestyle, those who workout can shift their attitudes from how it makes them look to how it makes them feel. *That's the key*, to focus on how exercise makes you *feel*. Moreover, just as athletes do, we can place a high value on what the body can do and have our appreciation grow in that area. Simply put, it's up to us!

As we've discussed, there is nothing wrong with appreciating and accepting physical beauty, since God created beauty, including the people he created. But we should strive to place our emphasis on functional body image, as I believe God would rather us do. And keep in mind that functional body image can extend to our minds too. That is, it's common for people who believe in God to acknowledge that God created our minds to seek out and know him. This is something that is possible because we have a body (with a brain)!

ACTIVITY 12

Word Association

Often when we here a common word, other words come to mind. For instance, if you hear the word "music," you might think of the word "song" or "instrument." If you hear the word "strong," you might think of "athlete" or "bodybuilder." This is known as word association, and it often indicates particular emotional traits about the person playing it.

So let's give it a try!

1. What are your first thoughts when you see the following terms:

Fat _____

Pretty _____

Slim _____

Thin _____

Yoked/jacked _____

Beautiful _____

Handsome _____

2. Now let's play word association with how *you* look. Which words (from the ones provided above or others you can think of) would you use to describe your own body?

_____

_____

_____

_____

_____

3. How many of your responses from no. 2 have to do directly with your body's physical traits (how you look)? How many have to do with your body's ability to function (what your body can do)? How many are positive? Negative?

_____

_____

_____

_____

_____

4. Something to reflect on about word association: While your answers to these questions can be interpreted in a variety of ways, consider what your first thoughts of your body were with each word. Would your first thoughts be pleasing to God? Why or why not?

_____

_____

_____

_____

_____

Catholic Aerobics: The Body and Sunday Mass

D id someone ever say something that was clever or funny, and you thought to yourself: "Man, I wish I thought of that first!"

That's what I thought when I heard the term "Catholic aerobics." Being an exercise physiologist (and practicing Catholic), I was a little envious when I heard someone say it. "Catholic aerobics" is an expression used to describe the many physical movements that take place during a traditional Catholic Mass. And there are a lot of them!

This next activity will probably challenge you, but let's try something. Your task is to get a partner and think of every physical action needed to fully participate in the Holy Mass, as well as note the part of the Mass in which this is done.

Here's an example of the first movement once we enter the Church:

Movement/Action	When/Part of Mass
Genuflect before the Blessed Sacrament	Prior to entering the pew

1. With your partner, provide as many other actions as you can and when they occur once the Mass begins:

Movement/Action	When/Part of Mass

2. Now have a group discussion to determine which movements (and when) you missed or forgot.

3. In a way, participating in Mass is a long prayer. Considering our personal prayer life, list some physical actions you can think of that are associated with various forms of prayer.

_____

_____

_____

_____

_____

4. If we were only spiritual beings, how would this impact attending Mass and our personal prayer life? That is, why is it important to engage in "Catholic aerobics" and have the ability to use our body in prayer?

_____

_____

_____

_____

_____

Clothes and Feelings

People of all ages know that the clothes we wear have an impact on how we feel about our bodies. Some prefer cold-weather climates so they can wear long sleeves and pants, even baggy clothes, while others prefer warm weather apparel for a variety of reasons, including comfort, style, and the option to "show some skin." Without question, clothing has a lot to do with our discussion on body image. Let's take a look.

1. Place the different set of clothes/outfits you wear into categories. For example: comfy, being "cool," casual, dressing up, preppy, cute, etc. Then, write down how those particular clothes make you feel.

Set of clothes/outfit	How it makes you feel

Set of clothes/outfit	How it makes you feel

2. What are some clothes that make you feel body conscious? When and why do you wear these clothes?

_____

_____

_____

_____

3. What types of clothes that other people wear make *you* feel body conscious? At the beach/pool? At a social gathering in the summer? Out socially?

_____

_____

_____

_____

_____

4. Regarding clothes/outfits, explain why you have different feelings in the summer than in the winter? Or is it the same? Why?

_____

_____

_____

_____

_____

_____

5. Are there occasions/events that you would like to avoid since they may impact your body image in a negative way?

_____

_____

_____

_____

_____

_____

6. Someone once said, "Wear the same thing to a party that you would wear if your pastor came for dinner." Explain why this is important to our discussion on body image. Be sure to include how the way we dress impacts other people. Why might it be unfair to other people to dress a certain way even if you are comfortable doing it?

_____

_____

_____

_____

_____

_____

Snow White and Superman

Materials needed:

- Computer and access to the internet (suggested)

When you first turned to this activity and read "Snow White and Superman," you probably thought: "Why on earth are we discussing Disney characters and superheroes when doing an activity with body image?"

And it's a good question.

But there is a strong relationship between the animated world and body image. Put simply, many animated characters, especially princesses and comic book heroes, are depicted in such a way that they probably have some impact on making its viewers/readers feel a little self-conscious about their own bodies.

With this in mind, answer the following questions on your own or with a group. If you are able to use the internet to look at a few of the suggested images, please do so.

1. Do an internet search for an image of Disney princesses (if you don't have the internet available, simply picture them in your mind). List three thoughts you have as you look at

these images or think about them. What similarities do they have in regards to their appearance? How might these princesses impact the body image of girls? What does it do to the way boys view girls?

_____

_____

_____

_____

_____

2. Do an internet search for a cartoon image of common superheroes, such as Batman and Superman, or for today's action figures, like G.I. Joe (if you don't have the internet available, simply picture them in your mind). List three thoughts you have as you look at these images. What similarities do they have in regards to their appearance? How might these characters impact the body image of boys? What does it do to the way girls view boys?

_____

_____

_____

_____

_____

3. While there is nothing inherently wrong with liking princesses and action heroes, what dangers do you see from what you wrote down in the first two questions?

_____

_____

_____

_____

_____

4. The saints are real life princesses and super heroes. Discuss some of your favorite saints and the virtues they can teach you. How can they help you build up your "spiritual muscles"?

_____

_____

_____

_____

_____

ACTIVITY 16

The Comparison Game

The Social Comparison Theory is a fancy term for something that probably happens every day. It's the experience of comparing ourselves to the people we see—whether those images are real life, actors in TV shows or movies, or the models in magazine/internet photos. Research suggests that the more images we see and the longer we look at them, the more those images remain in our minds and the more we compare ourselves to them. And you can probably see why researchers are interested in this; all sorts of powerful companies want marketing research to see how to best sell their products to you and your friends.

1. Can you relate to the Social Comparison Theory? That is, do you find that you compare yourself to others—whether in real life or in photos? Or is this not an issue with you? Explain.

_____

_____

_____

_____

2. Let's get specific: What are you doing when you find that you are comparing yourself to others (e.g., at school, the mall, working out, looking at a magazine)? Make a list of situations in which this comparison occurs. As part of the list, place the situations in order that have the most impact on comparing yourself to others.

_____

_____

_____

_____

_____

3. Consider the list you made in the previous question: Which are most avoidable and why? Which are the most difficult to avoid and why?

_____

_____

_____

_____

_____

4. Considering the impact that the Social Comparison Theory has on body image, what are specific actions you could take to avoid the constant need to compare yourself to others? Be sure to include in your list the ways that your faith would help.

_____

_____

_____

_____

_____

ACTIVITY 17

Reality TV

Just about everyone watches TV. While some of it can be educational and helpful to our physical, emotional, and even spiritual life, much of it is for entertainment purposes, and some can have a very negative effect on our life outlook and world view. That goes for your entire moral and spiritual life, but for our purposes here, it can certainly affect your body image. Let's investigate this further.

1. Name your three favorite TV shows.

_____

_____

_____

2. Name three current reality TV shows designed to appeal to teens and young adults.

_____

_____

_____

3. How many of your responses from no. 2 are the same as the responses from no. 1? List which ones.

_____

_____

_____

4. In general, who are the typical contestants on reality TV shows (provide details on race, age, physical attractiveness, etc.)?

_____

_____

_____

_____

_____

5. Why do you think these shows go after the characteristics you listed in no. 4?

_____

_____

_____

_____

_____

6. Do reality TV shows have a greater impact on your body image than, say, reading magazines, watching other types of TV shows/movies, or being social and going out with friends? Explain why or why not? In general, discuss the different feelings you have regarding your body image when you're watching these types of shows.

_____

_____

_____

_____

_____

_____

_____

What's Healthy?

Everyone wants to be healthy, both physically and emotionally. But there are factors that keep us from doing that. When it comes to our physical health, the reasons for neglecting our bodies are endless. Some don't have the time, others don't really know how, and some simply don't value the change.

Being emotionally healthy is even more complex. It seems to depend on a series of factors that include our upbringing, genetics, our current relationships, and as I would strongly argue, our relationship with God.

Although determining your overall well-being can be difficult, let's engage in a simple set of tasks to start.

1. List three actions or traits you do or have that identify you as physically healthy.

_____

_____

_____

2. List three things you do or don't do that identify you as physically unhealthy.

_____

_____

_____

3. List three actions or traits you do or have that identify you as emotionally healthy.

_____

_____

_____

4. List three things you do or don't do that identify you as emotionally unhealthy (if you don't feel comfortable sharing this with the group, keep this answer private).

_____

_____

_____

5. Reflecting on your responses for numbers 1 and 2, how can your relationship with God and your Catholic Faith (e.g., the sacraments) strengthen your body image? Explain, and be specific.

_____

_____

_____

_____

_____

6. Reflecting on your responses for numbers 3 and 4, how can your relationship with God and your Catholic Faith (e.g., the sacraments) help your emotional health? Explain, and be specific.

_____

_____

_____

_____

_____

Myth or Truth

Let's take a quiz!

Body image is a particular issue—similar to dieting and exercise—that has a lot of myths surrounding it, and this would be a great time to address those myths.

Answer True or False to the following. Then, we'll discuss each individually.

_____ 1. African Americans and other minorities do *not* struggle with a poor body image.

_____ 2. Only young adults and teens struggle with a poor body image.

_____ 3. Athletes are more likely than non-athletes to have a positive body image.

_____ 4. "Pretty" girls and "handsome" boys rarely have a poor body image.

_____ 5. Those who have a negative body image usually have an eating disorder.

_____ 6. Body image will improve if you change your body (lose weight, cosmetic surgery, etc.).

_____ 7. Those who have a poor body image in their teens will always struggle with this issue.

_____ 8. The media should take full blame when it comes to body dissatisfaction.

_____ 9. Most high school boys who take anabolic steroids to gain strength and size are athletes hoping to get a scholarship in their sport.

_____10. Obese boys and girls have much lower self-esteem than their non-obese peers.

1. African Americans and other minorities do not struggle with a poor body image.

False. For reasons not fully understood, some people think that a poor body image is only a "white people problem." The fact is, while studies on some minority groups such as African Americans demonstrate a more positive body image than their white counterparts, every race and nationality can suffer from a poor body image.

2. Only young adults and teens struggle with a poor body image.

False. There's no doubt that young people have the poorest body image than any other age group. But people of all ages and both sexes have a percentage who don't like the way they look. Some studies even show that women can struggle with body image issues well into their seventies.

3. Athletes are more likely than non-athletes to have a positive body image.

True. You might remember this fact going back to activity 13 when I discussed a study regarding functional body image vs. aesthetic body image. Athletes tend to have a more positive view of their bodies since they see it as a tool to get things done. Plus, many athletes are in good shape. When that's combined with the view that the body is a vehicle of functionality, the result would likely be a good body image.

4. "Pretty" girls and "handsome" boys rarely have a poor body image.

False. But seems impossible, huh? Often young people see being attractive as a major reason for happiness, but researchers speculate that *some* attractive people see the body as something to perfect, and thus have anxiety over even small imperfections, as well as the need to stay attractive. In other words, the expectation to stay attractive is a burden. Aging (and even just the thought of aging) can ruin someone's view of themselves.

5. Those who have a negative body image usually have an eating disorder.

False. The statistics spell this one out. Let's take teenage girls first. Some studies show that as much as 70 percent of teenage girls suffer from body distortion, whereas 10 percent have an eating disorder. For teen boys those figures are 33 percent and 2 percent, respectively. Note, however, that almost all who have an eating disorder would likely have issues with body image as well.

6. Body image will improve if you change your body (lose weight, cosmetic surgery, etc.).

False. While making changes like gaining some tone in your muscles or having liposuction will improve the way you look, and may even make some temporary minor change in your body image, most studies in this area show that such alterations will have little impact on how you see yourself.

Further, since body dissatisfaction is a complex issue, and mainly an emotional one, it seems clear that it's our mind that we have to change and not our bodies. But remember, starting an exercise regimen and diet program are great ideas; they should just be done to improve your health or make you a better athlete.

7. Those who have a poor body image in their teen years will always struggle with this issue.

False. In fact, this question gives me joy to answer. What I mean is that people tend to focus on different issues as they age, thus thinking less about how their body looks. Think about people in their twenties and thirties who are married and have children. Their concerns usually are on getting jobs that can buy a decent house and get a reliable car, and being a good mom and dad to their children. Plus, when they age, people start accepting aging (and changes in their bodies) as something that is natural and approved by God.

8. The media should take full blame of body dissatisfaction.

Trick Question: Neither. While most experts agree that the number one reason anyone has a poor body image is the bombardment of photographs in magazines, reality TV shows and movies, and other media, researchers have determined otherwise. They say action figures and superheroes (especially for younger children), hanging out with others who are fascinated by toned beach-bodies, and economic status all play a role as well. But no researcher in the area of body image has confidence that any set of reasons can point to anyone's poor body image issues. In other words, this issue is so complex that no one knows for sure what is the 100 percent cause of it.

9. Most high school boys who take anabolic steroids to gain strength and size are athletes hoping to get a scholarship in their sport.

False. One nation-wide study showed that 10 percent of high school boys took anabolic steroids, but most were non-athletes. This study, of course, is a reflection of how serious an issue body image is in our society. This demonstrates that male high schoolers have taken full notice of pro athletes and older recreational body builders and feel they will be accepted by their peers as well as desirable to women *only* if they gain a certain amount of muscle.

10. Obese boys and girls have much lower self esteem than their non-obese peers.

False. Actually, the percentage of obese vs. normal weight teens is more similar than you would expect. While this may be surprising to some, the reason for this makes sense. As just discussed in the response to question 8, body image issues are very complex, and while being overweight can add to the problem, no one can know for sure why someone has a poor body image. What remains clear is that God made us, he has a purpose for us, and we should seek him when trying to assess the value of our bodies.

What Have We Learned?

Throughout this workbook, you have been challenged to reflect on a lot of things concerning body image. Some activities focused on the causes of a poor body image, while others asked you to consider how God fits into the picture of how we see ourselves.

Whether you have engaged in a workbook like this or not, you are probably like a lot of young people in that you are often reminded that you are not just a soul. In fact, we have bodies, and especially in our culture, our bodies are signs of health, beauty, age, appeal, and talent, as well as many other things. But that's only part of the role our bodies play. God has something to say about this too.

To some degree, you will probably be forever challenged to see your body in the way that God intended. This final activity will provide an opportunity for you to think about some of the ways that this book may have helped you as you move forward in life.

1. Retake the survey from activity 4. Now that you have retaken the survey, reflect on your new answers (if there are any) and list three of most important lessons you've learned about body image.

_____

_____

_____

_____

2. List three specific things you could do to view your body as God intended.

_____

_____

_____

_____

3. List three things you could do to avoid having a negative body image.

_____

_____

_____

_____

4. Remember in activity 12 how we played Word Association? Look back at those pages, specifically your responses to questions 2 and 3. If you were to answer those two questions again, how would your responses have changed after reading this book?

_____

_____

_____

_____

_____